JUDGMENT

Jim Sweeney
Diana Bourisaw

EYE ON EDUCATION
6 Depot Way West, Suite 106
Larchmont, N.Y. 10538

ISBN 1-883001-37-4

Library of Congress Cataloging-in-Publication Data

```
Sweeney, Jim, 1937-
    Judgment : making the right calls / Jim Sweeney, Diana Bo urisaw.
       p.    cm.
    Includes bibliographical references.
    ISBN 1-883001-37-4
    1. School management and organization--Decision-making.
2. Judgment.  3. Critical thinking.  4. Problem solving.
I. Bourisaw, Diana, 1956-    . II. Title.
LB2806.S88   1997
371.2--dc21                                              97-19037
                                                            CIP
```

Production services provided by:
Bookwrights
1211 Courtland Drive
Raleigh, NC 27604

Published by Eye On Education

THE SCHOOL LEADERSHIP LIBRARY
INSTRUCTION AND THE LEARNING ENVIRONMENT
by James W. Keefe and John M. Jenkins

INTERPERSONAL SENSITIVITY
by John R. Hoyle and Harry M. Crenshaw

LEADERSHIP: A RELEVANT AND REALISTIC ROLE FOR
PRINCIPALS
by Gary M. Crow, L. Joseph Matthews, and Lloyd E. McCleary

MOTIVATING OTHERS: CREATING THE CONDITIONS
by David P. Thompson

ORAL AND NONVERBAL EXPRESSION
by Ivan Muse

ORGANIZATIONAL OVERSIGHT:
PLANNING AND SCHEDULING FOR EFFECTIVENESS
by David A. Erlandson, Peggy L. Stark, and Sharon M. Ward

RESOURCE ALLOCATION
by M. Scott Norton and Larry K. Kelly

OTHER LEADERSHIP TITLES
ADMINISTRATOR'S GUIDE TO SCHOOL-COMMUNITY
RELATIONS
by George E. Pawlas

THE EDUCATOR'S BRIEF GUIDE TO COMPUTERS IN THE SCHOOLS
by Eugene F. Provenzo, Jr.

HANDS-ON LEADERSHIP TOOLS FOR PRINCIPALS
by Raymond Calabrese, Gary Short, and Sally Zepeda

LEADERSHIP THROUGH COLLABORATION: ALTERNATIVES TO
THE HIERARCHY
by Michael Koehler and Jeanne C. Baxter

THE PRINCIPAL'S EDGE
by Jack McCall

THE PRINCIPAL AS STEWARD
by Jack McCall

FOREWORD

The School Leadership Library was designed to show practicing and aspiring principals what they should know and be able to do to be effective leaders of their schools. The books in this series were written to answer the question, "How can we improve our schools by improving the effectiveness of our principals?"

Success in the principalship, like in other professions, requires mastery of a knowledge and skills base. One of the goals of the National Policy Board for Educational Administration (sponsored by NAESP, NASSP, AASA, ASCD, NCPEA, UCEA, and other professional organizations) was to define and organize that knowledge and skill base. The result of our efforts was the development of a set of 21 "domains," building blocks representing the core understanding and capabilities required of successful principals.

The 21 domains of knowledge and skills are organized under four broad areas: Functional, Programmatic, Interpersonal, and Contextual. They are as follows:

FUNCTIONAL DOMAINS
Information Collection
Problem Analysis
Judgment
Organizational Oversight
Implementation
Delegation

PROGRAMMATIC DOMAINS
Instruction and the Learning
Environment
Curriculum Design
Student Guidance and
Development
Staff Development
Measurement and Evaluation
Resource Allocation

INTERPERSONAL DOMAINS	CONTEXTUAL DOMAINS
Motivating Others	Philosophical and
Leadership	Cultural Values
Interpersonal Sensitivity	Legal and Regulatory
Oral and Nonverbal Expression	Applications
Written Expression	Policy and Political
	Influences
	Public Relations

These domains are not discrete, separate entities. Rather, they evolved only for the purpose of providing manageable descriptions of essential content and practice so as to better understand the entire complex role of the principalship. Because human behavior comes in "bunches" rather than neat packages, they are also overlapping pieces of a complex puzzle. Consider the domains as converging streams of behavior that spill over one another's banks but that all contribute to the total reservoir of knowledge and skills required of today's principals.

The School Leadership Library was established by General Editors David Erlandson and Al Wilson to provide a broad examination of the content and skills in all of the domains. The authors of each volume in this series offer concrete and realistic illustrations and examples, along with reflective exercises. You will find their work to be of exceptional merit, illustrating with insight the depth and interconnectedness of the domains. This series provides the fullest, most contemporary, and most useful information available for the preparation and professional development of principals.

Scott Thomson
Executive Secretary
National Policy Board for Educational Administration

If you would like information about how to become a member
of the **School Leadership Library**, please contact:

Eye On Education
6 Depot Way
Suite 106
Larchmont, N.Y. 10538
(914) 833-0551 Phone
(914) 833-0761 Fax

ACKNOWLEDGMENTS

Writing a book about a subject as complex as judgment is no small feat. During the period in which this book was written, we wrestled with an incredible number of judgment calls in our 50,000 pupil urban district and even changed jobs and locations; Jim became an Interim Superintendent and Diana moved to a different state and an exciting superintendency. These are not optimum conditions for writing a book. Special people and great support made the effort possible. Jan and Steve, our great spouses, supported us spiritually and otherwise. Their love, encouragement, and help kept us going. Gail Jones and Jean Kawahatsu, wonderful secretaries and friends, contributed in many, many ways. Finally, the respect and caring we have for one another enabled us to learn from each other, support one another, and have some fun in the process.

ABOUT THE AUTHORS

Jim Sweeney, Interim Superintendent of Sacramento Unified School District, received his Master of Education degree in school administration from the State University of New York at Plattsburgh and his doctoral degree in education from Virginia Polytechnic Institute and State University. He served as a teacher and high school principal in upstate New York. During his 15 years as a professor at Iowa Sate University, Jim provided leadership for the field-based preparation program for principals and worked with principals across the country to improve schools. His publications and presentations include articles, booklets, and seminars on school leadership, teacher evaluation, and school culture and climate.

Diana Bourisaw, Superintendent of Fox C-6 School District in St. Louis, Missouri, received her Master of Education degree in special education from Northeast Missouri State University and Ph.D. in educational administration from Iowa State University. Diana has been a teacher, middle school principal, consultant, and school board member in urban, rural, and suburban settings. She has written and presented on such topics as site-based decision making, teacher evaluation, mentoring, and integrated instruction.

PREFACE

Perhaps the most damaging indictment against a principal is that he or she lacks judgment. A principal may lack a sense of humor, may not be the most academically talented individual in the school community, may habitually dress out of style, or by nature be a plodder in leading the school. Yet he or she may survive on the job for a long time and, with a little help from his or her supporting cast of teachers, students, and parents, may even be considered successful. But if the principal develops a habit of poor judgment, most observers would agree that he or she has given up the right to run the school.

Judgment in leadership is what makes any organization a predictable context so that those who operate in it and come in contact with it can proceed in an orderly fashion in fulfilling their organizational roles. In a school, good judgment on the part of the principal is a fundamental requirement for support of an orderly learning process.

The successful principal consistently exercises good judgment. Sound judgments are reached in a logical manner, are responsive to the problems that have been raised, and are made in a timely fashion. Judgment identifies priorities and responds to problems in order of priority. Judgment supplies the criteria for choosing and implementing proposed solutions.

Jim Sweeney and Diana Bourisaw give practical advice for making high quality judgments, based upon the experiences of many principals and other school administrators. They explain the important function of judgment in solving problems and provide many real life examples and practical tools for exercising judgment in identifying, prioritizing, and solving problems. At the end of each chapter they ask principals to personalize the material that has been represented and to reflect on its implications for the development of their own judgment skills.

The authors make the point strongly in Chapter 3 that sound judgments are based upon solid thinking skills. They assist readers in identifying their own thinking styles and in consciously using different styles and strategies in their approaches to different school problems. They demonstrate the need for deep thinking about school problems and encourage principals to adopt this type of thinking as part of their regular behavior as they approach even what seems to be routine problems in the school.

In Chapter 4 the emphasis shifts to the role of reasoning in making sound judgments. The complementary roles of inductive and deductive reasoning are explained, and the importance of formal logic in making judgments is developed. Potential roadblocks to reasoning are described, and tips are given for overcoming them.

Chapters 5, 6, and 7 focus successively on three related steps in solving school problems. First, the authors consider the ways in which problems can be identified and framed. They then look at the importance of generating alternative solutions and the role of creativity in the generation of alternatives. Finally, they describe a process for making the best choice from among the alternatives.

The book concludes with two chapters that provide assistance and direction for action. Chapter 8 provides a practice case that applies the skills and learnings developed in the first seven chapters of the book. The reader is systematically brought through the process by which judgments are made in resolving the problem presented by the case. The final chapter provides final thoughts and strategies for making sound and timely judgments.

Without the ability to make such sound and timely judgments, the principal will certainly fail. This very practical book provides the principal with clear direction for strengthening that critical skill.

David A. Erlandson
Alfred P. Wilson

TABLE OF CONTENTS

1

JUDGMENT

Judgment: Reaching logical conclusions and making high quality, timely decisions based on the best available information; exhibiting tactical adaptability; giving priority to significant issues.

Picture the following situation. It promises to be one of those days. You are in your office preparing to deal with two of the most important problems that you have confronted as a school leader. As you glance at your trusty planner, you notice there are other messy things on your "Do" list. You add these to the problems that will be flown in by telephone and others that typically find your office daily. It is a bit overwhelming. It would be nice to have some help with all of this. Suddenly you remember the judgment book that is in your bookcase, the one that has those reminders. You grab it and review the section on problem screening. That is helpful. You also review the sections on Level 2 Thinking and Reasoning and then make a copy of the Problem Mapping Guide. You are ready to get after it, feeling better and more in control. That is what this book is about; taking control of decision making and developing a most important skill—the ability to make judgment calls when solving problems.

Judgment is one of the 21 domains the National Policy Board for Educational Administration (NPBEA) identified as a functional skill needed to be effective as a principal (Thomson, 1993). NPBEA classified these domains into four groups:

FUNCTIONAL DOMAINS
  Information Collection
  Problem Analysis
  Judgment
  Organizational Oversight
  Implementation
  Delegation

PROGRAMMATIC DOMAINS
  Instruction and the Learning
    Environment
  Curriculum Design
  Student Guidance and
    Development
  Staff Development
  Measurement and Evaluation
  Resource Allocation

INTERPERSONAL DOMAINS
  Motivating Others
  Leadership
  Interpersonal Sensitivity
  Oral and Nonverbal Expression
  Written Expression

CONTEXTUAL DOMAINS
  Philosophical and
    Cultural Values
  Legal and Regulatory
    Applications
  Policy and Political
    Influences
  Public Relations

The domain classifications were developed to provide direction to those responsible for principal preparation and development. It is obvious that these 21 domains are highly interconnected and interdependent within and across classifications. *Delegation,* for example, is a way in which a principal chooses to exercise *leadership.* But skills within the interpersonal domain, such as *sensitivity,* are crucial in delegation and must be aligned with *philosophical and cultural values,* which are contextual. Judgment has a powerful impact on each of the domains; it is the essential skill. We make that case in this chapter and then provide opportunities to develop the skill.

Making judgment calls is the most important activity in which a principal engages. It begins the minute you wake up in the morning, accelerates when you enter those peaceful doors of that place called school, and continues until your mind says "good night." You are an active participant in the hectic, exciting, and often stressful business of making judgment calls. Here are some examples of the kinds of judgment calls that principals tell us they make daily:

◆ A mother wants to take her daughter out of school but you have received a call from her ex-spouse telling you not to allow the student to leave the school.

- Two students come into your office and ask if it is all right if they bring their friend to school tomorrow.

- Your most challenging (and marginal) teacher comes in and says that she wants to head up the literacy effort.

- A board member calls and suggests you get tougher on students who are doing poor work.

- You and your faculty have been studying the pros and cons of a block schedule for more than a year. You are really excited about what the block schedule can do for your school, but there is no consensus. Twenty or so of your ninety teachers strongly support the change. More than a third of your teachers are skeptical and want the change studied for another year. You also have a few teachers who strongly oppose the change.

It is important that we define the animal. The definition provided frames our thinking about judgment as it applies to the principalship:

Judgment: Reaching logical conclusions and making high quality, timely decisions based on the best available information; exhibiting tactical adaptability; giving priority to significant issues.

Our goal is to help you to make high quality, timely decisions. We will encourage you to use your intuition, but high quality decisions typically are a result of logical thinking and systematic application of basic principles. High quality judgment calls are tactical because they help you and your school advance toward your vision. Some judgment calls are rather trivial, while others are obviously more important. Some affect the elements less connected to instruction and student learning; others impact it directly. Some calls are easy; others are excruciatingly difficult. Most of the tough calls are strategy calls; they directly impact your mission and goals. Finally, the milieu in which you devise this strategy is swamp-like. You make tough judgment calls in a highly ambiguous and complicated institution that is part of a constantly changing ecosystem.

Let us examine your current state. How effective are you in making judgment calls? Take a minute and complete the following quiz to check your Judgment Quotient (JQ).

Perfect Principal Quiz

Please read each statement and check (✓) if you agree (A) or disagree (D) with the statement.   A   D

1. I never have such messy problems that it is difficult to determine cause and effect, or the relationship between all the pieces in the problem puzzle.   ___ ___
2. I have a perfect process for solving problems. ___ ___
3. My emotions do not affect my judgment.   ___ ___
4. I never do the wrong ethical or moral thing.   ___ ___
5. Possibility or creative thinking is easy for me in solving all my problems.   ___ ___
6. It is easy for me to find or take time to just sit down and reflect on my work.   ___ ___
7. I make the right decisions 90% of the time.   ___ ___
8. I do not have any work-related problems.   ___ ___

If you agreed with seven or more statements, close the book and call (916) 264-3055. We have never met a perfect principal; we will attempt to clone you. If you agreed with six or more, call (916) 264-3055; you are an expert and we need your help. If you responded "disagree" to a number of statements, you are very honest with yourself and can profit from this book. What you will learn will sharpen your judgment saw and enhance your problem-solving effectiveness.

WHY IS JUDGMENT IMPORTANT?

Much has been written about the effective principal. Early attempts at description included behaviors such as "monitors curriculum" and "evaluates teachers." Later versions included more lofty ideas such as "visionary." While instructional leadership activities are important and while vision provides you a desirable destination, ask yourself if either could be achieved without good judgment. The principal cannot monitor the curriculum, evaluate teachers, or be visionary without making good judgment calls. Truisms are statements of truth that are well known. Next is the first of what we call Reminders. We will use these reminders throughout the book.

Reminder

Judgment separates the less effective from the more effective principals and has a powerful impact on school effectiveness.

Good judgment calls result in decisions that improve things for you and students in your school. They are based on analysis of the information you can reasonably gather in the time you have and are designed to put you in a position to improve your school. Good judgment calls put "first things first." The bottom line is that making judgment calls is what you do as a school principal. It will make or break you.

What does research tell us about principal effectiveness in decision making? In truth, there is little information about principal judgment, but a survey by the American Management Association determined that business people make the "right decision" only 20% of the time. Let us assume that you are more than twice as effective as the average businessperson and make a good decision 50% of the time. Here is the perfect way to save time: flip a coin every time you have a tough decision. We hope you have a three-year contract.

We also hope you are beginning to see things our way. Even if you tend to agree with us, you are probably still asking the $64,000 question, "Why should I read this book?" and, "how will it help me?" We wrote this book because most principals tell us they do understand the importance of making good judgment calls and would like to get better at it. They say they would like to acquire the tools and skills they need to improve their judgment. But very few are able to describe the process they use in making judgment calls. Most say they just mull things over and then decide. Some say they have never really thought about judgment and the role it plays. Improving judgment, like the improvement of any complex skill, requires conscious attention. This leads to another reminder.

Reminder
If you always do what you have always done, you will always
get what you have always gotten.

To get better at anything, to develop or refine any skill, we must change what we are now doing and adopt new ways of thinking and behaving. To develop your judgment skills and apply them in the real world, you must first understand the essential elements of judgment and then have a firm grasp of how to use them to be more effective. This book will help you to understand those elements and provide you tips for improving your skill in making judgment calls. It is time to repeat the obvious. Judgment is a learned skill. If you read this book, apply what you learn, and continue to practice and work on the skill, you will make better judgment calls. You will be more effective and experience less stress. Here is the first big judgment call you must make to get better. Check the line provided if you want to improve your judgment. If you are not ready to make that commitment, read more of this book until you are.

___ *I commit to reading and thinking about judgment and to doing whatever it takes to improve my judgment.*

OBJECTIVES AND LESSON PLAN

A book, like a lesson, is designed to instruct. Good lessons have clear and specific goals or objectives. The purpose of this book is to help the reader to:

♦ Utilize a systematic approach in making decisions and solving problems.

♦ Improve judgment in making decisions and solving problems.

♦ Reflect on practice and further develop thinking skills and judgment.

This book will be of value to any people interested in improving their judgment and solving problems, but principals and soon-to-be principals are our primary audience. Whether you read this book as part of a course or seminar, or if it is something you turn to on the weekend or during the summer, it will provide some specific information that will help you in the real world.

Judgment is a complex subject. It makes some sense to break it down into segments or pieces, but no sense to leave it that way. In this book we attempt to break it down and then reassemble it. You are about to complete Chapter 1. We hope you have figured out that we wanted to set the stage by reminding you of the importance of judgment as well as give you a flavor of the book.

This reminder anchors the approach and contents of this book:

Reminder
Good judgment is a result of effective thinking, effective information processing, and the systematic use of a problem solving method.

Judgment demands effective utilization of the skills required to collect, analyze, and synthesize information; thinking skills that enable you to connect and weigh problem factors; and a systematic way to reason your way to a good choice. Chapter 2 provides a foundation; the judgment-action model, problem solving pitfalls and the seven-step problem solving framework are presented. Chapter 3 focuses on effective thinking and provides tips for thinking smarter. Chapter 4 is about reasoning or how to use intuition and logic to make tough calls. In Chapter 5 we provide a framework and guidelines for scanning, screening, and focusing on the problem. Problem mapping provides a systematic way to analyze the problem. Chapter 6 provides a process and techniques to generate the best alternatives. Chapter 7 gets down to the details of making the very "Best Choices." Chapter 8 provides an opportunity to apply the information before you use it in the real world. In Chapter 9 important schemes and ideas are summarized for ready reference and suggestions for growth are provided.

HELPERS

A book is useful if it guides learning. Its format should help the reader understand, apply, and transfer learning. The following learning strategies will help you sort out, remember, and use (not lose) the "stuff" that enables you to make better decisions:

> *Activities.* The reader will be asked to write or perform activities to promote deeper thinking, promote use of the skill, or facilitate back home application.
>
> *Reminders.* These statements provide the basis for building a belief system.
>
> *Frameworks.* Throughout the book, theories and principles have been reduced to models that will help you to understand the material.
>
> *Key Behaviors.* These are behaviors that increase effectiveness in problem solving or judgment.
>
> *Reflections.* Questions are presented periodically to promote reflection.
>
> *Scenarios.* Scenarios are real situations that have occurred in our schools.

HOW TO GET THE MOST OUT OF THIS BOOK

There is an old saying, "forewarned is forearmed." For this book to improve your judgment you must be ready to "think about how you think." You must be prepared to be reflective while reading the book and to commit to reflection during and after practice. We will do what we can to encourage you to think about practice, as well as about how you think and behave in your work place. The rest is up to you.

Here is the drill. Read a chapter. Complete the activities, and do a self-analysis. Think about the ideas, and relate them to your world. Identify what you will do to improve your skills. Test and try the new approach. If it works, use it; if it does not, discard or refine it. Then read another chapter, and repeat the process. When you have completed the book, write down the specific things you will do to strengthen your judgment. You may wish to use this book in some other fashion. Do it in whatever way best accommodates your learning style. It is a judgment call.

FOR REFLECTION

Please reflect on the following questions or statements. Then write down your responses and put them in a place where you can refer to them as you read the other chapters.

♦ What are the toughest judgment calls you have to make and why are they most challenging?

♦ Identify the judgment call you are least proud of and describe why your judgment was not effective.

♦ What makes it difficult for you to make judgment calls?

♦ What do you most want to learn about judgment calls?

2

JUDGMENT AND PROBLEM SOLVING

All problems become smaller if, instead of indulging them,
you confront them. Touch a thistle timidly and it pricks you;
grasp it boldly and it crumbles.— William S. Halsey

It is riddle time. What do you do that you seldom think about that contributes more to your success and happiness than anything else you do? Surprise, make judgment calls! While you make hundreds of routine judgment calls weekly, it is the high-stakes judgment calls that require great expertise and skill. Selecting an innovation, identifying a teacher as marginal, or even changing your school start time are high stakes because they are high risks. Anything that threatens your job security or job satisfaction is high stakes. High stakes judgment calls are complex and ambiguous; they are "swampy" problems.

High stakes judgment calls typically involve trade-offs between several important goals where no best choice is clear. Changing a school calendar or arbitrating a standoff between a teacher and a student teaches you how tough it is to find common ground. Determining which teacher was at fault in a teacher-teacher dispute teaches you there are few facts and no high road on the trip you take daily. People problems are squishy, scary, and uncomfortable. The more people involved, the deeper the potholes. The more the problem involves values and emotions and people working together, the muckier it gets. Draining the swamp is impossible; you have to learn to move quickly through it because there is little time to amble around and check things out. In this chapter, we first explore the nature of problems and then discuss problem-solving pitfalls and the seven-step problem-solving framework. We then present a judgment model that describes a cyclical process with interaction between you, the environment, and the problem. Finally, we describe the features of the mental searching process you use in making judgment calls and the analytic/artistic approach needed to make judgment calls.

PROBLEM SOLVING

Problems. Problems. Problems. We all have them. An Olympic diver recently opined that, "It is not hard to identify problems when you are standing in front of 6 million people in only a small piece of lycra and you are about to jump off a board three buildings high." School principals have it tougher; they dive into swampy ground every morning. Problems come in various shapes, sizes, and levels of complexity and ambiguity. A problem is typically regarded as something unpleasant. Many equate a problem with a headache; it is bothersome, painful, and difficult to end. We ask you to think about problems in a different way. A problem is simply a deviation, imbalance, or gap between a desired state (should be) and a current state (actually is). Anything that needs to be made better is a problem. You probably agree, for example, that your goal as a principal is to provide leadership so that your school can become the best it can be. This entails improving student achievement for all children and targeting some children so that all students are achieving to their potential. That is the desired state. The gap between that desired state and the achievement level of students in your school is a problem. Solving problems is simply what you do to achieve excellence. While it is a productive activity, it does have its pitfalls.

PITFALLS

There are pitfalls to avoid as you make your way through the swamp. Listed here are some that are most common. Identify those most likely to trip you up.

Pitfall #1: Trying to Solve Problems That Are Ill-defined or Too Large. Even a true optimist is hesitant to attempt to solve the problem of world hunger. Yet, principals and others frequently define problems in world hunger terms. "Improving student achievement" is not a problem statement, it is a mission statement. A problem must be defined in terms that narrow its scope and provide sufficient specificity to be attainable and measurable.

Pitfall #2: Jumping to a Solution Before Really Analyzing the Problem. Principal Lynn, a first year principal, learned that there were discipline problems in the school. Lynn made a judgment call: institute in-school suspension. It is absolutely amazing how many principals fire and then aim. It is important to act quickly, but it is more important to act correctly. Can you identify a solution without understanding the problem?

Pitfall # 3: Tackling Problems Beyond Your Control. Principal Marty decided that her problem was the grievance procedure in the master contract. Marty then set out to change the contract. That may be a good long-term strategy, but it is probably beyond Marty's control. It is very important to delimit the problem so that it has a realistic chance for implementation.

Pitfall #4: Applying Pet Solutions. Teachers in Principal Chris's school are upset about students' failure to complete their homework. Chris learns that teachers are not doing a good job communicating with parents so he implements the homework hotline that was so successful in a former district. Chris's pet will not be too successful in this situation; they tried the hotline before he was principal and teachers and parents did not like it. Most of us have our pet solutions to recurring problems; however, most problems demand unique solutions. Leave your pets home.

Pitfall # 5: Failure to Consider Situational Aspects. There is a need to implement a school improvement approach in Upandatem Elementary. Principal Sandy decides to use the effective school model and to bring in a consultant to enhance the readiness of the staff. It does not work well. (It was a disaster!)

The staff is ready for change but thinks the effective school approach is restrictive and disempowering. Sandy should have collected information about the situational aspects before making this judgment call.

Pitfall # 6: Level 1 Thinking. Upandatem Elementary has an opportunity to become a magnet school. Principal Jamie talks to teachers and others and analyzes the situation. There are many positives. She will lose two relatively new teachers but thinks it is worth it. Jamie decides to move forward. After receiving the grant Jamie learns that the teachers are very angry because of the loss of these two teachers whom she did not realize were so popular. Jamie only got to Level 1 in her thinking. She identified the positives and some of the negatives but did not think deeply enough to consider the impact of the loss of these other teachers. Had Jamie gotten to Level 2 Thinking by massaging the information and thinking deeply about it, she would not have made a bad judgment call. The swamp is a tricky place. It makes you think—and rethink—at a deeper level. You will learn more about Levels 1 and 2 Thinking in Chapter 3.

THE SEVEN-STEP PROBLEM-SOLVING FRAMEWORK

We have discussed ambiguity, complexity, levels of thinking, information processing, and how problems make the terrain swampy and fraught with pitfalls. It is time to begin to make our way through the swamp. The best way to avoid problem pitfalls and deal with swampy problems is to break down the problem-solving process into simple steps and attack them. A number of books and articles address the steps in problem solving. *Step-By-Step Problem Solving* by Chang and Kelly (1995) is short and sweet and very helpful; we highly recommend it. The Seven-Step Problem-Solving Framework (Figure 2.1) reflects the way in which we believe problems should be solved. It also provides a framework for judgment. You may not need to follow each of the seven steps in every problem-solving situation. If you have defined the problem (step 1), for example, you move to step 2. There may be times when you retrace your steps to be sure you get it right.

FIGURE 2.1 THE SEVEN-STEP PROBLEM-SOLVING FRAMEWORK

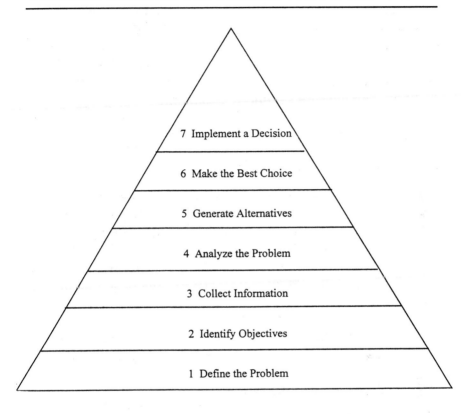

7 Implement a Decision

6 Make the Best Choice

5 Generate Alternatives

4 Analyze the Problem

3 Collect Information

2 Identify Objectives

1 Define the Problem

STEP 1. DEFINE THE PROBLEM

Have you ever been lost? Solving a problem is like finding your way when you are lost. It can be exciting or terrifying. A problem sometimes is like a stone in your shoe. You know something is in there but you are not exactly sure what it is. Problems are not easily defined; you usually get the best definition of a problem after you have found the solution. The key to defining a problem is to be specific and to delimit the problem so that you are not working on a solution to world hunger.

STEP 2. IDENTIFY OBJECTIVES

Problem solving and judgment are about results. The only way to achieve anything—small victories or major triumphs— is to identify what you want at the outset. Identifying the problem objective enables you to have a target upon which to focus your efforts. You will improve your problem-solving skills by at least 25% if you ask the Results Question below when solving problems.

Results Question: What will be the outcome if I successfully solve the problem; what will be the result?

STEP 3. COLLECT INFORMATION

Information is the oil that enables the problem-solving mechanism to function. Without information the thinking cylinders will be scored. Solving a problem without sufficient information is like traveling cross country without a compass or map. If you omit important information or collect invalid information, you cannot effectively conduct the next step in the problem-solving process nor make good judgment calls.

STEP 4. ANALYZE THE PROBLEM

The extent to which a problem is effectively and efficiently solved is a function of problem analysis. Complex and ambiguous problems are a tangle of conflicting factors. You need to know what the key factors are and how they relate to one another. Can you correct a morale problem if you do not know the factors involved, including its background or history? Determining the cause(s) of the problem is important but not the bottom line. As strange as it sounds, the solution is not always derived from identifying the problem alone. Take it even a step further; fixating on the cause of the problem can obscure the solution. A fairly typical school situation is illustrative. If the teachers are very negative about participating in a staff development activity initiated by central office because they had little input and have a relatively high distrust of central office, the solution cannot be linked to the cause because you are unable to do anything about the cause. The solution will depend on your ability to generate alternatives.

STEP 5. GENERATE ALTERNATIVES

Step 5 is important and requires the maximum level of creativity. You cannot get a $100 solution from $50 alternatives. The only exception to that is if you put two $50 alternatives together. The solution to complex problems usually requires more than one alternative. Thus, a simple Reminder.

Reminder
More and better alternatives result in better decisions.

Better alternatives result from focused attention, possibility thinking, and skill. There is more to it than simply brainstorming. You will learn more about how to generate alternatives in Chapter 6.

STEP 6. MAKE THE BEST CHOICE

How many times have you divided your yellow pad and listed the pros and cons of various alternatives? Many of us have used the Franklin Method (refer to Chapter 7) to determine the alternative that best satisfies needs. It is not a bad approach, but you can do it better. In Chapter 7 we discuss how to identify criteria and weigh the various elements to make the best choice.

STEP 7. IMPLEMENT A DECISION

The road to ineffectiveness is paved with good intentions. Analyzing the problem is the most difficult step in decision making, converting it into effective action is usually the most time-consuming one. Decisions about actions that include who, what, when, and how must be built into the decision itself. Even the best decision has a relatively high probability for being wrong. The very best decision tends to become obsolete. While it is important to collect and examine information, the best way to monitor a decision is to determine if it is working.

These seven steps are interconnected. For example, gathering and organizing information appears as the third element but is an ongoing activity throughout the problem-solving process. The key to successful problem solving is to develop skills in each of the seven steps and practice them until they become part of how you think and behave when you solve problems. We want you to have a mental picture of these seven steps and be able to quickly apply them in the day-to-day business of solving problems. In Chapter 4 we discuss how a basic pattern of problem solving that utilizes the ability to reason results in judgment calls.

THE JUDGMENT-ACTION MODEL

Models help us to understand how the components of a complex activity are connected. The model in Figure 2.2 is an adaptation of Hogarth's (1980) model. Eight elements interact as you make judgment calls. Let us apply the model to your world and begin with the *task environment*. Problems do not occur in a vacuum. Every problem has a context, a set of surrounding factors that interact with the problem and influence elements of the problem. Failure to collect, process, and analyze information to understand the task environment and to stay tuned to changes in the environment is a sure recipe for failure.

Every action you take in the process of making a judgment call is affected by your *problem orientation,* the attitudes and ways of thinking you bring to that problem. Let us assume, for example, you are faced with a high-stakes problem in which you have to decide what teacher to assign to a very challenging group of at-risk students. These students need a teacher who really understands them and is sensitive to their needs. It is high stakes because of the impact on the kids and because your board is very concerned about teacher assignments to at-risk students. One major aspect of your orientation to this problem is that you believe that younger teachers are more apt to be successful with at-risk kids than are veteran teachers. That has been your previous experience, and you have heard other principals express the same view. With that problem orientation you then move to *information utilization* which has three subelements, *information collection, information processing,* and *information analysis.*

Information utilization begins with *information collection.* Judgment calls are all too frequently muffed because of availability bias; the person making the judgment call simply processes whatever information is available and does not seek information that would have cast the problem differently. You cannot make good judgment calls without answering "yes" to two big questions: Do I have the requisite relevant information needed to analyze the problem? Is the information current and accurate? The first question is a fancy way of asking if you have the important information you need to analyze this problem. In the situation involving the assignment of a teacher, you need to have sufficient information about the students to know what teacher attributes or characteristics are needed to help those students succeed. You need to know what teachers are available and the skills and attributes of those teachers. It would surely be helpful if you knew something about their preferences and attitudes. If you have sufficient experience in the building, you can access much of that information through recall; your memory bank is one of your best information sources. If your experience in the building or knowledge of your teachers is limited, you will have to get it elsewhere.

The best decision makers collect information better than their peers. They identify the appropriate sources and means to answer the big questions: WHAT? WHO? WHEN? WHERE? and WHY? When you decide that you have sufficient important information given the time you have, you move on, keeping your eyes and ears open and asking questions. The quality of a judgment call is dependent on the quality of information you have at the time you decide. Always ask yourself if you trust the information you have collected.

When you have collected sufficient accurate information you engage in *information processing*. There are three elements in the information processing puzzle: sorting, integrating, and prioritizing. If you want to know how much money you have in a big piggy bank, you first sort coins to make counting easier and more efficient. So it is with information. In the at-risk problem, you process the information more effectively if you separate student information from the teacher information. Your brain can process like information more effectively; it gets confused when processing bits and pieces from several aspects of a problem. In the at-risk assignment this is relatively easy, but in more complex problems sorting is challenging. After the information is sorted and some analysis done, it must be integrated. For example, after you collect the information that tells you about the students in the class, determine the common characteristics. The power to reason enables you to solve problems that goes far beyond instinct or any technology that people have created. Chapter 4 provides more information about reasoning. Finally, there is a need to prioritize the information so that you can deal with the most relevant pieces and discard information you do not need. The best way to do so is to scan your mental screen and block on those things that are most important. Then cut and paste them to the top of your screen. When they have been sorted and prioritized, move to the final step, *information analysis*.

Information analysis requires that you make decisions about the task environment, classify the problem, determine its importance, and identify probable causes and other factors that affect the problem. You also collect information to generate alternatives to solve the problem, then make the *judgment call*, and move to *action* by implementing it. That action produces an *outcome*. In the at-risk problem, that outcome is likely to be reflected in the satisfaction of the students and parents, in discipline referrals, and in other indicators of success. Outcomes feed back into the task environment and influence your problem orientation. The judgment-action model describes a sequence of activities that is dynamic because of the interactions between its elements and cyclical because each outcome feeds back into the process.

Figure 2.2 The Judgment-Action Model

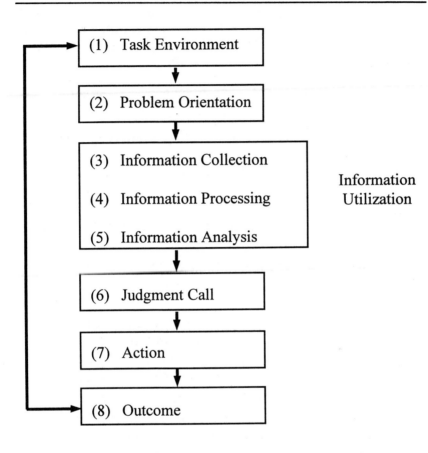

BASIC FEATURES OF MENTAL PROBLEM SOLVING

Problem solving is a mental process. We follow a routine in thinking through a problem. The identified features are a modified version of Ruchlis' (1990) conception of basic problem-solving patterns:

1. The judgment call draws on *past experience* and *facts* that have been incorporated in the mind.

2. Facts and ideas that apply to the problem are recalled by a *mental searching* process that digs into the huge fund of memories stored in the brain. Somehow, in a manner not fully understood, we are able to direct our minds to search out those facts that apply to the situation and thereby leave out the multitude of other facts that are not of value in solving the problem.

3. Facts and ideas that apply to the problem are identified by *scanning* or seeking information from relevant sources.

4. Facts and ideas that apply are then *juggled* in our minds to *understand the problem* and to evolve different possible solutions. The process of putting together the facts to try out *thought experiments, reason correctly,* and *draw conclusions* is the essence of judgment.

5. A chain of such reasoning activities examining possible solutions finally ends with an overall conclusion. We *mentally evaluate* each situation and render a *judgment*. We select one or more alternative solutions we think or feel will be most successful.

6. Finally, we take action to solve the problem. That is the basic purpose of judgment and the ultimate test of good reasoning. The best action, of course, is for the action to solve the problem. But, if not, all is not lost. We put that outcome—whether a success or failure—into our memory banks as *an experience*. The next time in a similar situation, that experience may be drawn upon to speed up this business of making judgment calls.

To summarize, (Figure 2.3) your brain begins the judgment process by mentally searching your memory bank, selecting relevant facts and ideas stored from previous judgment calls and discarding those that do not add facts or ideas relevant to the problem. The brain then scans the environment and identifies information it has forgotten and new information. When it has been determined that your brain has sufficient information, it moves to the next step. It juggles the information to better understand it. That is, it organizes and connects ideas and facts so that it can be analyzed. The next mental step is to try out some thoughts and see if they lead to sensible conclusions using a process of reasoning. You then use these conclusions to think your way to identifying possible problem solutions, evaluate those choices in light of the situation, and make a judgment. This judgment leads to a successful or unsuccessful outcome. This success or failure is deposited and stored in your memory bank waiting for the next mental search.

ANALYTICAL-ARTISTIC APPROACH

Are the use of the judgment-action model and the judgment mental process a science or an art? Is judgment a science or an art? The literature on decision making reveals that approaches range from tightly analytic (quantitative decision trees) to loosely intuitive (oughts and shoulds). Neither end of the pole offers much; making high-stakes judgment calls requires analytic and intuitive skills. A decision-making approach, like a good martini, has the proper proportions. Our approach is heavier on the scientific side, but in a friendly manner. The seven-step framework reflects the scientific method and is systematic. The tactics and strategies we propose for use in the seven steps require use of basic principles, procedures, and skills while remaining sufficiently flexible to allow you to use them in your own way. There is a place for intuition in decision making but we must be clear as to what is meant by intuition and when and how it is used. Intuition is that feeling in your gut or flash of insight that tells you what to do.

Despite the allure of gut feelings and flashes, research tells us they do not consistently produce good high-stakes decisions.

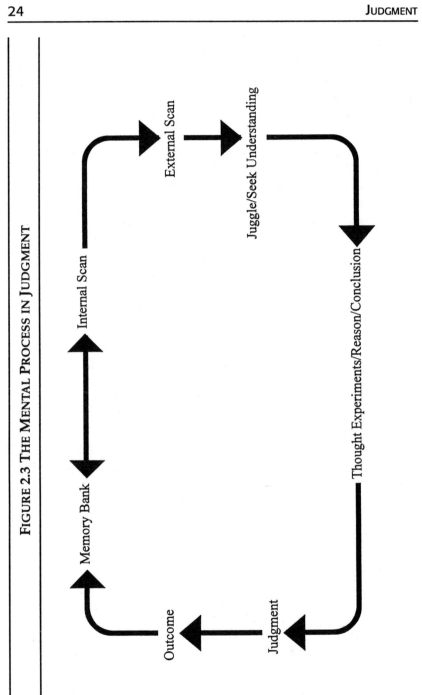

FIGURE 2.3 THE MENTAL PROCESS IN JUDGMENT

Over 100 studies have compared intuitive judgments to an objective standard, and not one has found intuitive judgments to be superior (Mowen, 1993). It appears that sound procedures result in better choices than feelings and flashes. But many good, and some great, high-stakes decisions are made by relying on gut feelings. This apparent contradiction needs explanation. Intuition, for the most part, results from expertise. The highly expert decision maker simply has a larger and better organized data base and scans, juggles, thinks, reasons, and evaluates more quickly and more effectively than the novice. Intuition is not magical, it is learned. The great decision makers use their expertise and skill like a great artist painting a landscape. They learn their craft until they can practice it seemingly without effort, and they get wonderful results. Our approach in this book is to provide you with the information needed to practice your craft and achieve those same results.

KEY BEHAVIORS

Do . . .

+ consider the context of the problem environment.
+ think of problem solving as information collection, processing, and analysis.
+ write down the problem-solving framework and use it until it becomes a part of your thinking.
+ write down the mental searching process and use it until it becomes a part of your thinking.

DON'T . . .

- try to solve a problem that is poorly defined or too large.
- jump to the solution before analyzing the problem.
- tackle problems beyond your control.
- automatically use a solution that worked in your last district.
- be a Level 1 thinker.

FOR REFLECTION

♦ Go back and examine the judgment-action model. What are the new ideas about which you are going to think?

♦ What problem-solving pitfalls are most likely to plague you?

♦ Review the seven steps in the problem-solving framework. Find a way to frame them in your mind so that you can quickly recall them when you solve problems.

3

THINKING

Thinking is the ultimate human resource.
—Edward de Bono

It takes much more than a sharp machete and a strong body to work your way through the swamp. From the moment you walk into your office and pick up your "Do" list, thinking is the most important leadership activity in which you engage. The more complex the challenge, the greater the need to think well. *Think* about the next Reminder and ask yourself to what extent you agree with us.

Reminder
Your most important skill is your ability to think your way to excellence.

Is thinking an inherent act like walking or breathing or an acquired skill like driving a car or roller skating? Thinking is like roller skating. If you line up a group of individuals and they participate in a roller skating race, you quickly learn who has the most natural ability. If, however, you provide all the participants opportunities to become better roller skaters, most participants will go farther and faster than before, and those who invest the most will move up in the pack. You want to move up in the pack or you would not be reading this book.

This chapter will increase your understanding of the thinking process and enhance your thinking effectiveness. We begin

27

by discussing effective thinking and then paint a profile of the effective thinker. The 4 C Thinking Wheel helps you better understand how to think more effectively when solving a problem. We then discuss the thinking styles that characterize both sides of the brain and provide an opportunity to assess your thinking style. An explanation of de Bono's Six Hats provides specific ways to use your thinking skills in problem solving. Level 1 and Level 2 thinking are discussed. Finally, because leadership in schools frequently involves emotion, we discuss how emotions affect your thinking and provide suggestions to help you stay calm, cool, and collected when solving problems.

EFFECTIVE THINKING

Effective Thinking (ET) is the operating skill that utilizes intelligence and experience to solve problems. Thinking is active and functional. It draws on both natural or innate intelligence and the knowledge and thinking skill acquired through experience. The brain provides a broad, if unequal, spectrum of thinking attributes. These attributes, which some equate with intelligence, include creativity, memory, preciseness, and analytical skill plus attributes that are part of your developing personality. Following are five attributes that characterize effective thinkers. Check yourself out.

Confident. ET is confident of his thinking. This confidence revolves around a perceived ability to turn on his thinking and deliberately focus it in the direction needed plus the ability to think through complex and difficult matters and reach good solutions. ET has experienced success in problem solving and is almost cocky about his ability to think through tough problems.

Humble. If ET steps over the confidence line, failure will be right alongside. Arrogance is a major thinking sin. When a thinker begins to believe she has *the* answer she stops thinking. Be confident in your thinking but humble enough to keep thinking.

Self-analytical. ET consistently practices reflective thinking. ET assesses her skills and identifies strengths and shortcomings.

Open. ET welcomes ideas and new ways of thinking. ET treats an idea like a flower regardless of whose garden in which it is growing. Ideas are nurtured and valued.

Controlled. ET manages the thinking process and emotions. ET stays focused, exercises self-discipline, and maintains objectivity.

To what extent do these five attributes describe you? Which attributes are your strongest and which need strengthening? Identify one attribute in need of strengthening and identify things that you will do to develop that attribute more fully. Write them down and begin tomorrow.

My strongest attribute is _____

One attribute I would like to strengthen is _____

_____

I will take the following steps to strengthen this attribute:

1. _____

2. _____

3. _____

4._____

THE 4 C THINKING WHEEL

The 4 C Thinking Wheel (Figure 3.1) provides a vehicle for continuously improving your thinking. It is an adaptation of the "Shewhart Cycle," a powerful tool for improving quality embraced by the business sector. This cycle, also known as the PDSA (plan-do-study-act) cycle, provides a process for continuous improvement. It utilizes John Dewey's concepts of reflective thinking and the Wheel of Learning conceptualized by Senge et al. (1994) in *The Fifth Discipline Handbook*. The wheel provides a way to take deliberate action in employing the thinking process while problem solving. Use the wheel to improve the way you think when solving problems.

FIGURE 3.1 THE 4 C THINKING WHEEL

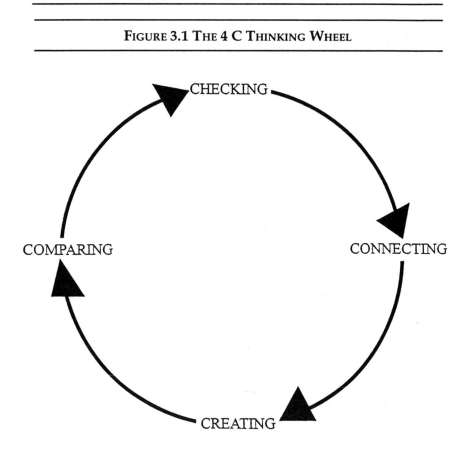

Checking

The first step in preparing yourself for problem solving is to check your thinking and determine what you need to do to prepare yourself to think effectively. Start with an examination of your mental and emotional approach to the problem. Principals tell us that, sometimes, when they need to make a very difficult and important decision, they are too stressed, frazzled, or tired to think through the problem effectively. When you are faced with a challenging and important problem, be sure to examine your state of mind. If you are angry, frustrated, scared, or distracted, determine what you need to do to enable yourself to think effectively. We will provide some tips to help you with this later in this book. Next, ask yourself if you have certain beliefs or assumptions that bias you to the extent that you cannot effectively collect, analyze, or evaluate information. If that is the case, find a way to check that baggage in long-term parking and do what is needed to clear your mind, bring focused attention to the problem, and think effectively.

There are several key checking behaviors to utilize:

♦ Clear your desk and mind. Visualize how you are now thinking and how you must think to be effective.

♦ Identify the emotions, attitudes, or mental elements affecting your thinking and what you will do to ensure that you are thinking effectively.

Connecting

Think "Big Picture." In this phase you identify the elements of the problem and connect them. Like a scientist generating hypotheses, think about relationships and connections between people, actions, events, and results related to the problem. Begin thinking about cause-and-effect relationships and what to do to solve the problem. The key connecting behaviors include:

♦ Identify the people, actions, or events that appear to be connected.

♦ Identify the relationships between people, action, and events.

◆ Frame the Big Picture.

◆ Determine cause and effect.

CREATING

It is possibility thinking time. Problem solving typically requires thinking outside the box. Possibility thinking kicks in and continues throughout the thinking process. Creativity and a sense of optimism spawn big or new ideas and ways to solve the problem. Create new solutions from old solutions. Use these key creating behaviors:

◆ Identify at least one out-of-the-box idea that might provide a better alternative and solution.

◆ Brainstorm ideas, actions, events, and people that help you to think of the best alternative.

COMPARING

As you continue through the 4 C Thinking Wheel you are continuously evaluating ideas. Evaluation becomes operational and intensifies in this phase. You choose criteria, weigh the relative value of ideas, and compare the potential benefits and consequences. Compare the value of ideas and decide which choice will yield the best outcome. Here are the key comparing behaviors:

◆ Use criteria to evaluate ideas.

◆ Identify and weigh negative and positive consequences.

◆ Compare alternatives and select those that will produce the best results.

Let us review. Check - Connect - Create - Compare. The 4 C Wheel describes a way to think when solving problems. *Checking* your thinking enables you to avoid the problem solving pitfalls and to go about the business of problem solving in an effective way. *Connecting* the pieces in the problem puzzle is the key to solving complex problems. Your mind thinks better when it sees the big picture. *Creating* produces the best ideas and solutions. *Comparing* is a most difficult but important step in determining the ideas that get best results.

BRAIN POWER

What has 10 billion nerve cells and can store more information than all the libraries in the world? Your brain; that magic human machine that stores information, manages the information processes, creates ideas, and controls the reasoning process. Much has been written about the brain and how it functions. Because both the brain and the computer organize and process information, the brain is frequently compared to the computer. At first blush, the computer appears to be much more effective. The computer stores huge amounts of information. Given the proper cues, it categorizes information very quickly and well. It does not forget. However, your brain is far superior to a computer in many ways. Even the most powerful mainframe computer is relatively useless when confronted with messy problems. It is worthless when confronted with value judgments. Computers are also unable to sense a problem or see the big picture. Your brain enables you to encounter ambiguous situations and deal with them in a logical manner. It helps you generate exciting alternatives. Your brain is very special. Let us examine how the brain works in solving problems.

TWO SIDES TO THE STORY

According to the old proverb, "There are two sides to any story," and your brain is no exception. The brain has a right and a left hemisphere. Research indicates that typically one side of the brain is dominant and that we are more likely to exhibit the characteristics of that side in daily behavior. We are even more likely to exhibit dominant brain tendencies under stress. Examine the characteristics of the left and right brain, read the descriptions that follow, and determine whether your right or left brain dominates your thinking style:

Left Brain — Language, logic, numbers sequence, look at details, linear, symbolic, representation, judgmental;

Right Brain — Images, rhythm, music, imagination, color, whole patterns, emotions, non-judgmental.

Both sides of your brain house specialties that help you think effectively and make good judgment calls. Your left brain houses your logical and analytical skills; your right brain houses the visual, pattern-making, intuitive skills. The left brain files and processes hard data, facts, and details. The right brain handles or processes your emotions, images, and intuitive traits; when you get angry or sad your right brain processes the stimuli that resulted in that emotion. While recent studies have revealed there is some crossover, it appears that most of us have two distinct information processing sides. Your right brain imagines and creates. It enables you to see and generate alternatives. It sees the big picture and triggers this magic quality called intuition. You use your left brain to reason, to think logically. You also use it to organize information and to synthesize and evaluate that information. Solving problems requires both logical thinking and creativity. The trick is to be sure that you are making maximum use of both sides. It helps to know your natural or dominant style so that you can understand your thinking tendencies, particularly under stress.

YOUR THINKING STYLE

While there are those who have balanced thinking styles, most people have a preferred or dominant thinking style. Understanding that style not only helps you understand how you think under stress, it provides an opportunity for growth and improvement of your performance. The key to effective thinking is flexibility; we must be able to use both sides of our brain in making high-stakes judgment calls. Below is the Thinking Style Check-up. Complete the check-up and determine which side of your brain controls your thinking.

THINKING STYLE CHECK-UP

Circle the response that you believe best represents your beliefs, attitudes, or behavior.

1. In a problem-solving situation, which would you be more likely to do?
   a. mull over solutions, then discuss them
   b. recall past experiences that were successful and implement them

2. Concerning hunches, you:
   a. have hunches and follow them
   b. occasionally have hunches but do not place much faith in them

3. Do you usually have a place for things, and use a system to organize things?
   a. yes
   b. no

4. When you have to speak without warning at a meeting, do you:
   a. just talk
   b. make an outline

5. When preparing for a difficult task, do you:
   a. plan and prepare notes
   b. visualize yourself accomplishing it

6. Do you make choices because they feel right or based on information?
   a. feel
   b. information

Here are the scoring procedures for the check-up. List the numbers of each answer you checked.

1a=7	2a=7	3a=1	4a=7	5a=1	6a=1
1b=3	2b=3	3b=9	4b=1	5b=9	6b=9

Now add the number of points you scored and divide by 6. For example, if you scored 36 points, you would have an average of 6. Now place your score on the brain preference continuum.

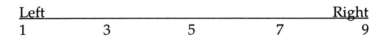

Left				Right
1	3	5	7	9

This quiz gives you an indication of your brain preference. There is nothing good or bad about your tendency. If, however, you are highly right or left brained, it will be difficult to make good judgments unless you make a conscious effort to achieve balance. If you are right brained (close to 9), you tend to be overwhelmed by emotions and the feeling of the moment. These emotions block out logic and rational thinking. High right brainers might quickly decide to tell off the superintendent . . . or worse. If you are highly left brained (close to 1), you are very linear and not inclined to see the big picture or connections between the pieces in the puzzle. Extreme left brainers are capable of recommending sterilization to solve the population problem. The bottom line is that you do not want to be either a 9 or a 1; some balance will give you the best results. But what you really need to do to increase your problem-solving effectiveness and judgment is to stretch your thinking style so that you use both your left and right brain to think your way through problems. Following are suggestions for stretching your thinking styles.

LEFT BRAINERS - STRETCHING TO THE RIGHT

♦ Think of a problem that needs solving. Generate a minimum of 20 possible solutions. Do not stop to analyze each solution, just write down the solutions.

♦ Select two of the above solutions. Picture these two in your mind. Visualize the implementation of these solutions.

♦ Create a song about one of your solutions.

♦ Draw a picture about your solution.

- Envision where your successful solution takes place. Visualize your solution taking off in a plane, having a successful flight, and landing smoothly on the runway.

- Take a walk. Think green thoughts. Look at all the greenery around you. Visualizing green helps expand your mind and generate ideas.

RIGHT BRAINERS - STRETCHING TO THE LEFT

- Pick up a local newspaper. Sit down and complete the crossword puzzle; it will help you to practice sequencing and promote orderly thinking.

- Identify your most pressing problem. Give yourself sufficient time to generate some solutions. Number and prioritize these solutions. Write a memo to your staff about this issue. Write down what you learned from doing it and what you will do in the future.

- Outline your solution. Identify the steps in the process. Write these steps down. Read them to yourself and ask yourself if they make sense and will work.

- Think caution to slow down and consider the consequences.

- Plan a social activity. Organize the event. Identify possible sources for failure of the event.

SIX THINKING HATS

There are other ways of characterizing thinking styles that help clarify how we think when problem solving. De Bono's Six Thinking Hats employs left and right brain thinking characteristics to solve problems. De Bono contends that confusion is the biggest deterrent to clear thinking. When confronted with a high-stakes problem, we try to do too much at once. Emotions, logic, information, creativity all crowd in on us and give us far too many balls to juggle. De Bono's six different thinking hats provide us an opportunity to intentionally do one type of thinking at a time. Using Six Thinking Hats helps us make decisions about which hat to wear as we go through the problem-solving process. Next is a simplified explanation of de Bono's Six Thinking Hats. Examine the Hat descriptions and identify ways to remember when and why to wear each Hat.

1. *White Hat.* White is a neutral color. Think of a white sheet of paper with information on it. That sheet is neutral, it simply provides the information you need to make a judgment. When you do White Hat Thinking you are information collecting. You cannot think your way through a problem without the information needed to solve the problem. Four key White Hat questions can guide you prior to making a judgment call.

   ◆ What information do I have?

   ◆ What information is missing?

   ◆ What information do I need?

   ◆ How do I get the information?

2. *Red Hat.* Emotions are an important part of the problem-solving process; they give relevance to our thinking by fitting our thinking to our personal needs and the emotional aspects of the situation. We need to be in touch with our emotions and to understand the extent to which they are involved in our thinking. The Red Hat has to do with feelings, intuitions, hunches, and emotions. When you put on your Red Hat, you acknowledge and legitimize your emotions and feelings and determine to what extent these feelings legitimately should be reflected in your thinking and the judgment call. Here are three key questions for Red Hat Thinking.

   ◆ What emotions or feelings are involved in my thinking?

   ◆ Should I include or exclude my emotions or feelings in making this call and to what extent should they play a role?

♦ What do I need to do to ensure I am thinking objectively?

3. *Black Hat.* "Here comes the judge." The black hat is for evaluating and judging and is one most of us are comfortable with. When you wear the Black Hat, you look on the black side of things and do it in a logical way. The Black Hat enjoys identifying and explaining why something will not work. If you often play the Devil's Advocate role and enjoy it, you are likely to be a Black Hat thinker. Evaluation is a major element in making judgment calls. Throughout the problem-solving process you are putting on and taking off your Black Hat. Three key questions play an important role in Black Hat thinking during problem solving.

♦ To what extent is this information, including my assumptions about relationships, accurate, valid, and sufficient?

♦ What is wrong with this alternative?

♦ What could go wrong with this choice?

4. *Yellow Hat.* Yellow is for sunshine and brightness. You put on your Yellow Hat to find ways to solve the problem because you are optimistic; you can find a way. You are creative when you wear your Yellow Hat. Your thinking revolves around how it can be done to enjoy the benefits. Three key questions drive the Yellow Hat Thinker.

♦ Why not do this?; it will work.

♦ What great things will happen as a result?

♦ Why isn't everybody for this?

5. *Green Hat.* Think plants and growing. Green is the color of fertility and symbolizes growth. The Green Hat believes that great things grow from tiny seeds. The Green Hat thinks about growing and creating ideas and alternatives. Key questions include:

- ◆ What are the big ideas?
- ◆ How do we make them happen?
- ◆ What are the possibilities?

6. *Blue Hat.* A blue sky covers everything. Blue symbolizes coolness and control. The Blue Hat is for process control. The Blue Hat thinks about how she or he or the group is going about solving the problem. The Blue Hat thinks about process and also thinks about what hats are being worn. Key questions:

- ◆ How am I thinking about this problem?
- ◆ What process am I using to solve the problem?
- ◆ Where am I in the problem-solving process and how well am I doing with each step?

HAT USE

While one should not be overly prescriptive in how and when these hats are worn, it makes sense to provide some guidelines as to their use. Consider these suggestions for use of the Six Thinking Hats.

White Hat	Use early in problem solving but leave on throughout.
Green Hat	Use when generating alternatives.
Red Hat	Leave off most of the time but use when needed.
Yellow Hat	Use when creating and tackling tough problems.
Black Hat	Remove when creating. Put on when examining choices.
Blue Hat	Do not go too long without putting on the Blue Hat. Check where you are and how you are thinking and problem solving.

HAT CHECK

Let us pause and do a brief self-assessment. Take a moment and write down the answers to the first four questions. Stop and reflect on your answers. When you have had time to reflect, respond to question five and find a way to translate your intentions into action.

1. What color hat do you normally wear?
2. Do you change hats as frequently as you should?
3. What color hat should you wear more frequently?
4. What color hat should you wear less frequently?
5. What will you do, using the Six Thinking Hats, to increase your effectiveness?

SYSTEMS THINKING

Systems thinking, popularized by Peter Senge (1990), has played a major role in changing or reworking many corporations. A system is a perceived whole whose elements hang together because they continually affect each other over time and operate toward a common purpose. In systems thinking, the pattern of interrelationships between key components defines the system. At the very heart of systems thinking is the assumption that a change in one part of the system produces a change in the whole structure. These connections may not be readily discernible or connected by time and space. The evidence to support this is overwhelming. A heavy fog closes the airport. People who were supposed to travel do not. Speeches are not given and business not transacted. These events impact other system elements. A more complete explanation of systems thinking is beyond the scope of this book. *The Fifth Discipline* (Senge, 1990) and *The Fifth Discipline Fieldbook* (Senge et al., 1994) provide us with three keys that are important in problem analysis and in making best choices:

1. *Think Globally.* While much of this book promotes linear thinking, you must think globally to identify the various problem factors and to make the connections between these factors.

2. *Think Dynamically.* Understand that system parts change very rapidly; change must be factored into problem analysis and solutions.

3. *Think Connectedly.* Understand that a change in one part of the system impacts other parts of the system with the end result being system change.

LEVEL 1 AND LEVEL 2 THINKING

Deep problems require deep thinking. The single most common mistake in problem solving is the failure to think deeply enough to solve the problem. As a result, we commit one of six errors that are directly attributable to thinking: (1) omit information, (2) fail to analyze information correctly, (3) draw false conclusions, (4) omit or fail to consider alternatives, (5) omit evaluation of consequences or improperly evaluate consequences, and (6) make improper selection of alternatives. While errors can result from bias or illogical thinking, they are more likely to emanate from the failure to think deeply enough to solve the problem effectively. There are no clearly defined levels of thinking; however, we find it helpful to frame them as Level 1 and Level 2. Following is a description of both levels and tips as to when and how to use them. Figure 3.2 shows the characteristics of the two levels.

Level 1. A teacher walks into your office and informs you that she will be unable to supervise the field trip scheduled for next week and that it would be dangerous to send the kids without her. She reports that she has spoken to many of the parents about this and they see no problem; the class can go later. You tell her to go ahead and cancel the trip. Sixteen hours later you are up to your elbows in alligators. At least a dozen parents have personally called you to tell you what a horrible person you are. Their kindergarten children are very disappointed, and the parents had taken time off from work to go with the students. The Mayor's wife is particularly miffed; the trip was her idea. Not to worry, however. They are going to the superintendent to get this terrible wrong righted. It is two-aspirin time. You sit and wonder what happened.

Level 1 thinking deserves credit for this mess. You collected very little information and saved your thinking skills for tomorrow. Level 1 thinking is the low-level use of information processing and thinking skills in making judgment calls. Figure 3.2 shows the levels of thinking and how they impact problem elements. When you are thinking at Level 1, you consider few of the situational and other key factors, think about the immediate situation and the short term, make some of the connections, consider fewer and lower quality alternatives, and are more likely to make a choice based on the feeling you get from thinking about the obvious benefits and unintended consequences of one or two alternatives.

Level 2. The Level 2 thinkers simply think deeper to consider many situational and key factors, think long term and big picture, and make the connections between factors to determine cause and effect. They then generate more and better alternatives and more effectively determine positive and unintended consequences. The Level 2 thinker examines consequences more effectively, generates more and better alternatives, puts it all together better, and weighs the choices more skillfully. The Level 2 thinker thinks more deeply to consider key factors and connections between factors (Big Picture) and also thinks long, not short term. But the most significant difference is that the Level 2 thinker examines the situation more deeply and is significantly more effective at determining the extent to which to apply past experiences and generalizations to the present problem. The Level 1 thinker is more likely to generalize inappropriately from successful and unsuccessful experiences or so-called proven practices in choosing an alternative. Put simply, what worked or did not work in the past, or what worked elsewhere may or may not be effective in solving your problem: IT DEPENDS ON THE SITUATION. The Level 2 thinker examines the situational factors involved in past experiences to determine to what extent they match the problem situation. Further discussion of how to examine and apply generalizations is provided in Chapter 4.

Level 1 thinking is appropriate and efficient when the problem does not require full use of the processes and skills. Most routine problems do not require that you think deeply about the

FIGURE 3.2 PROBLEM ELEMENTS AND LEVELS OF THINKING

	Context Scan	Key Factors	Time Frame	Scope	Connec-tions	Conse-quences	Alterna-tives	Evalua-tion	Application of Generalization
Level 1	Few	Few	Short Term	Snap-shot	Few	Few	Few, Low Quality	Feel, Simplistic	Surface
Level 2	Many	Many	Long Term	Big Picture	Many	Many	Many, High Quality	Weighing, Complex	Deep

situation or examine the long term and big picture. Unfortunately, many problems demand Level 2 thinking; situational factors make even routine problems unroutine. High-stakes problems require Level 2 thinking. You cannot afford to act like Aristotle when trying to decide what lunch schedule works best. Nor can you afford to make judgment calls like the one cited above. You have to be at Level 2 thinking and able to operate at it very effectively.

While that describes how Level 1 and Level 2 thinking impact how we solve problems, it does not explain how to become a Level 2 thinker. This book should help you figure that out. Suggestions for operating at Level 2 are presented in Chapter 9.

EMOTIONAL THINKING

Three pounds or so of cells and neural juices make you special and influence your thinking. Let us conduct a brief brain examination. The brainstem, which surrounds the top of your spinal cord, regulates basic life functions such as your breathing and metabolism. The brainstem neither thinks nor learns, it is preprogrammed to ensure your survival. The iambic or thinking brain resides in the top layers of your brainstem. The thinking brain has a neocortex which contains the hippocampus, thalamus, amygdala, and visual cortex. The hippocampus receives stimuli while the thalamus acts as a conduit sending stimuli to the amygdala. The amygdala is an almond-shaped cluster of interconnected structures that acts as an emotional sentinel or alarm. This alarm is not the same in all of us; the amygdala has "learned" how to react to emotional stimuli. While all of this happens very rapidly, your thinking brain gives you time to adjust to your emotions.

Goleman (1995) recently provided a startling perspective on the brain that has powerful implications. His research suggests that alongside this mind that reflects and then reaches conclusions is another system of knowing that is impulsive and sometimes illogical. It is the emotional mind and is influenced by the amygdala. The amygdala triggers wonderful emotions such as love and joy and some emotions not so wonderful such as fear and sorrow. Without the amygdala you would be unable to gauge the emotional significance of events. You would not experience love, hate, or joy. Remember, the cortex translates stimuli into meaning. When that translation goes to the amygdala it activates the emotional centers. Although it may produce anger that could color our judgment, we do have time to deal with it and minimize the negative effects on our judgment.

One of the most telling discoveries of the last decade helps us understand another way in which our emotional brain affects our judgment. LeDoux recently learned that portions of the original signal the thalamus received from the senses are not transmitted to your thinking brain; they go straight to the amygdala, triggering an emotional response before the cortex has had an opportunity to "think" about it. In these cases, the brain acts without thinking. Thus, you may "lose it" as a result of an insult before you have a chance to think about the consequences. The judgment that will eventually come into play in this situation revolves around what do to fix whatever problem your emotional brain got you into.

What is to be derived from all this brain theory? First, expect to have emotional reactions to various stimuli. Certain behaviors may cause you to experience anger and may cloud your judgment. Emotions can sometimes bypass the thinking process and result in unproductive or damaging behavior. Hopefully, these episodes will be few and far between. In the segment that follows we discuss how to stay calm, cool, and collected when making decisions, and in Chapter 4 we discuss emotional hot buttons and how to minimize their impact. The good news is that emotions can power your best thinking. Gary Kasparov, the great Russian chess master, was a passionate and aggressive champion. His passion is what fueled his desire to win. Later in this book, we will discuss focus, and how important it is to zero in on a high-stakes problem with great intensity. While emotions can fuel the will to win and focus great intensity on a problem, emotional thinking must be controlled.

CONTROLLING EMOTIONAL THINKING OR HOW TO STAY CALM, COOL, AND COLLECTED

It is Friday afternoon, and you have had a tough day. The cafeteria manager went home before lunch, three teachers called in sick but only two substitutes showed up, and two fights broke out before 10:00 AM. Your PTA has planned a spaghetti dinner for tonight and are expecting 400 people. Two of the three teachers who were scheduled have canceled already. Your secretary rings your office. The night custodian is on the phone. She says the high school quarterback has broken his arm and her second-string son is now starring in tonight's game. She would like the night off. You lose your cool. You blow up letting her know that her job comes first, the PTA is counting on her, and so are you. You slam down the phone with no resolution.

Sound familiar? Do you recall the last time you made a decision when you were frustrated, angry, or anxious? Did you make a good judgment call? Thirty percent of the time emotional judgment calls will lead to more negative consequences than if you were calm, cool, and collected in making the call. There are many things in your personal and professional life over which you have no control. Unless you run a private or magnet school you cannot choose the students who enroll at your school, nor can you choose the behavior of others. You can choose how you think about their behavior and how it affects your judgment. The formula for improving your behavior in these stressful situations is:

(-) Negative Feelings + (+) Effective Thinking =
(+) Productive Behavior

Reducing negative feelings and increasing your thinking effectiveness makes you more productive. But you must understand your negative feelings and what causes them. Some questions will identify events or interactions that interfere with your objectivity and how you typically cope with these events:

♦ When am I most likely to respond with anger? With tears? With fear?

♦ When am I most in control of my behavior?

♦ What steps have I taken in the past to regain control of my emotions?

♦ What steps have I taken in the past to prevent my emotions from controlling me?

Examine the list that you have generated. Take a yellow pad and write out the answers to the questions below. You may be able to complete them in one sitting, but it may require more research and thinking.

♦ What coping mechanism can you use to help you block out or reduce the emotions that get in the way of effective thinking?

♦ What can you do to minimize your emotions and maximize your effective thinking?

Mindmapping

A Mindmap is an idea map; it represents relationships between ideas using symbols or words. You can use the Post-It, that wonderful invention of 3M, to graphically represent connections and relationships. Main ideas are centrally located, with other relationships and interrelationships depicted. A Mindmap allows you to think about a subject from many angles and reinforces the visual learner. But even more importantly, it allows your brain to do what it does best, make meaning out of fragmented pieces. Your brain is much more comfortable discovering patterns than linear relationships. If you sit in your office and write your ideas down on those wonderful Post-Its and then put them up where your brain can scan them, that big picture view will stimulate Level 2 thinking. When you coordinate the big picture with its details, your right and left brain work as partners in whole brain processing. They are able to process, store, and recall information more efficiently. Mindmapping is further discussed in Chapter 9.

Key Behaviors

Do . . .

+ check your thinking from time to time.

+ connect pieces in the problem puzzle.

+ create solutions.

+ compare possible solutions.

+ use both sides of your brain.

+ wear the Six Hats appropriately.

+ be a systems thinker: global, dynamic, connected.

+ think at Level 2: many factors, long time, big picture, many connections, consequences and alternatives, holistic weighting.

+ identify a place to think.

+ keep a log of new strategies you have used in your thinking.

+ reduce negative feelings and rev up thinking for best results.

DON'T . . .

- solve a problem when angry, frustrated, depressed, etc.

- be arrogant about your thinking ability.

- make excuses about not having time to think.

FOR REFLECTION

♦ Write down what you will do to use the weaker side of your brain to solve problems more effectively.

♦ Identify the Thinking Hat you need to wear more frequently and what you will do to use the Six Thinking Hats.

♦ Write down two things you will do to get to Level 2 and think more effectively. How will you remember to use these strategies?

♦ When do you tend to think emotionally? What will you do to keep emotion from getting in the way?

4

REASONING

Elementary, my dear Watson.

A military officer at a nuclear missile base in the Arctic was faced with a problem that might even have appeared more serious than some that you face. He was sitting at a radar screen that showed a flock of missiles heading toward America. His hurried call to headquarters was not answered. It was his responsibility to determine if he should press the button that would send United States missiles hurtling toward Russia. It was a judgment call, perhaps the ultimate call in the history of the world. What would he do? The military officer decided to ask one final question in those final moments: Where is Kruschev? In New York City at the United Nations.

The judgment call: do not push the button. The reasoning that prompted him to ask that question and use the missing information saved the day—as it will for you in your job on a daily basis. The mental processing described in Chapter 2 also played a role in saving the day. Put yourself in the role of that military officer, and apply the mental process. First, conduct a mental search and come up with the information stored in your memory bank. Then scan the environment, pick up more information about the situation, juggle these facts and ideas, and conduct a thought experiment: Where would Kruschev be if the missiles were on the way to New York? Certainly not in New York! It is illogical that he would bomb himself. You conclude that some-

51

thing is wrong and take your finger off that button, a very good judgment call. Sounds simple, but it is not. Reasoning is complex and challenging. When handling a parent complaint or restructuring an element of the school program, you rely heavily on your capacity to mentally process information and to reason. This chapter describes the elements of reasoning and the reasoning process. Inductive and deductive reasoning and how to overcome reasoning roadblocks also are discussed.

REASONING

Reasoning is the mental ability to analyze and connect facts and ideas to reach a logical conclusion. Inductive and deductive logic are used to reach logical conclusions. When we form generalizations from many specific examples we use inductive reasoning or logic. Deductive reasoning is based on logic. If A is true and B is also true, then C must be true. It is important to understand how both help you to reason.

INDUCTIVE REASONING

Recently it was suggested to a principal that she meet with two parents who had expressed concerns about a recent change in procedures and were very critical of her decision. The principal, without thinking, chose to meet with each of them separately. When asked why she made that judgment call she explained that she instinctively knew that the parents would be difficult to deal with together, but if she met with them separately she would be able to connect with them and work through the problem. When asked how she knew that (without consciously thinking about it), she was not sure. Further probing revealed that her previous experiences with challenging parents had been less positive when more than one parent was present; she was more effective one-on-one. Information gained by experiences stored in her memory was triggered by the need to make a decision. You take stands on issues, develop meeting agendas, make personnel selections, and choose programs using inductive reasoning—and it works just fine. Very effective decision makers use inductive reasoning because it draws heavily on experiences and their human side. In a human business that is a big plus. But it does have a down side.

While generalizations are assumed to be true because they held up in other cases, their usefulness in the matter at hand is contingent on their representativeness of the instances observed. Therein lies the rub. First, many of these instances are profoundly affected by the interaction between situational variables. An approach that was successful with Mary may rub Bill wrong because of Bill's personality and the interaction of your personality and Bill's. In addition, the generalizations are often based on very few cases and are influenced by vividness and the recency of cases. Inductive reasoning has a place in judgment, but high-stakes calls also require deductive reasoning.

DEDUCTIVE REASONING

Deductive reasoning relies on logic. General Norman Schwartzkopf's televised Gulf War briefing illustrates how deductive reasoning drives high-stakes judgment calls. General Schwartzkopf and his staff systematically analyzed relevant requisite information and logically deduced a plan to destroy the enemy. The plan included contingency plans to deal with the unexpected. Inductive reasoning probably played a role in some of the decisions; General Schwartzkopf has conducted hundreds of trial runs and learned from them. But he was not about to risk the lives of thousands solely on his feel for the situation. Schwartzkopf and his staff reasoned their way to victory.

THE PROCESS

Reasoning is an information processing activity that draws on inductive and deductive reasoning. When you encounter a problem, you sense or deduce that something out there needs attention. You collect information, define the problem and its potential impact, and formulate objectives. If it is a high-stakes problem, you collect more information, juggle it and determine the most important factors, and generate and examine alternatives. You then develop some hypotheses (if I do X, then Y will happen) and weigh the potential outcomes and benefits. These steps are all part of the deductive reasoning process. The reasoning process and the mental judgment process are tightly connected. What makes them work is the use of formal logic.

FORMAL LOGIC

Logic is the science of correct reasoning. It is the heart of deductive reasoning. While we learned to think logically as children, knowledge strengthens the skill. When we reason, we employ these concepts: *assumption, premise, syllogism, inference, conclusion, hypothesis, and choice.* Definitions of these concepts are given below, followed by a discussion on using assumptions and generalizations to develop a premise for use in formal logic. A problem is then presented that illustrates how these seven concepts facilitate reasoning.

Assumption	Statement believed to be true.
Premise	One of two connected assumptions that lead to a syllogism.
Syllogism	Two connected statements that lead to a broader conclusion because of the suggested relationship between the premises.
Inference	Use of reasoning to reach a conclusion.
Conclusion	Judgment formed after examining the relationships between premises.
Hypothesis	If-then statement based on the conclusions reached.
Choice	Option chosen to address problem.

Formal logic is dependent upon the development of valid assumptions and premises, which frequently are derived from generalizations. A premise is a statement of fact or a supposition or assumption based on what one assumes to be true. Such truths are typically based on data, experiences, or information gleaned from others. Research provides the basis for many such premises or assumptions. Many of the premises, suppositions, and assumptions which leaders formulate are based on generalizations, suppositions, or conclusions reached by examining the results of other instances. In Chapter 3 we discussed the need for Level 2 thinking to make valid generalizations. Some examples of what happens when we do not think deeply in making generalizations are provided.

Superintendent Lynn has a problem; Lynn needs to get the Mayor and city council to support the bond issue. They have been less than lukewarm to this idea. Lynn has had major differences with them in the past and is looking for a strategy to get their active support. Lynn knows that one successful way to get congressional leaders' or senators' support is to flood them with letters from constituents. Lynn calls a meeting of the principals and shares with them a plan to have them and others write letters to the mayor and council members. They do, and the mayor and council members repudiate the bond issue. What went wrong?

The premise or assumption is that letters to public officials garner support. The superintendent generalized that this practice gets positive results. She failed, however, to consider the situational factors. She has a tenuous relationship with the mayor and city council. This is a local matter, not one where the participants do not know each other. The mayor and city council know many of the principals well. When they learned what the superintendent had done, they interpreted it as a devious way to pressure them, not simply as letters from constituents. While legislators know that constituent letters are frequently strategically manipulated, most see it as part of the democratic process and are not antagonized by it. The superintendent's failure to consider these situational factors and think deeply enough to discern important differences resulted in an inappropriate generalization, a false premise or assumption, and a poor judgment call.

Principal Pat accepts a position as principal of a relatively large school whose faculty has a reputation for perverseness and resistance to change. Pat reads the literature and talks to her professors to determine how to proceed. Based on research and information gathered, Pat concludes that the way to turn this faculty around is through tight supervision and implementation of the effective school process. At the first faculty meet-

ing, Pat informs the faculty that they will be examining effective school practices and they should expect visitations to their classes beginning the next week. This pronouncement is met by anger and threats which are followed by calls from the superintendent and board members. What went wrong?

The premise is that the effective schools process and clinical supervision will make a difference. It was generalized from research and from information received from others. Unfortunately, Pat apparently did not know that the last principal had tried a similar approach and the faculty rebelled. Pat's strategy added insult to injury. Pat needed to know the conditions under which the generalization was applicable and the conditions that were present in the school.

Some guidelines will help you make and apply valid generalizations to serve as premises in making logical decisions in high-stakes problems. They require Level 2 thinking:

♦ In forming a premise, verify the information or facts and identify the conditions under which past experiences have been successful or unsuccessful.

♦ Identify the key factors, connections, and other situational factors and reach conclusions about them and how they impact the problem.

♦ Match the generalization and conditions reached in Step 1 and the conclusions reached in Step 2 to determine the extent to which the generalization applies to the problem.

♦ Think deeply about the conclusions reached in each of the three steps, and formulate a premise that is valid.

The problem of books provides an opportunity to apply the formal logic process in making judgment calls.

The Problem of Books

Your school libraries are in poor shape; students do not have sufficient up-to-date and appropriate books to read. This is a great concern to you, your staff, and the community because more than 70% of your students' reading proficiency test scores are below grade level. Although your staff has recently engaged in excellent staff development to improve the teaching of reading and you have worked very hard to ensure curriculum alignment, reading scores have not risen as much as you expected or to an acceptable level. It has been suggested that more library books might make a difference. You must make a judgment call as to whether or not to spend a significant amount of money on books.

Using the steps in the deductive reasoning process, you collect and analyze data related to success in improving reading proficiency and examine your students' achievement data. Assume this data collection results in two premises.

Premise 1: Increasing the number of books that low socioeconomic (SES) students read has a positive effect on reading proficiency.

Premise 2: Most of your students are from low SES families.

Remember, a syllogism is developed by connecting the two premises. Because an increase in the number of books read significantly increases reading proficiency for disadvantaged students (Premise 1) and because most of your students are disadvantaged (Premise 2), you deduce the syllogism below and conclude that buying books will enhance reading achievement.

Syllogism: Increasing the number of books that disadvantaged students read has the greatest positive impact on reading proficiency of low SES students, and most of our students are disadvantaged.

Conclusion: Buying books is the most salient way to increase our students' reading proficiency.

Deductive reasoning led you to conclude that additional books will increase your students' reading proficiency. You made inferences to reach that conclusion. You inferred that the research is valid and assumed that the results of research conducted in other schools is generalizable to your school. Even if the research turns out to be faulty your reasoning is sound because you followed the rules of logic. While problem solving calls for reasoning much more complex than the syllogism above, the flow of logic employed in this example applies to many judgment calls. Use factual information to derive basic premises, check your facts and basic premises, and reach conclusions that are logically derived. It does not make sense not to use deductive reasoning whenever you are able to collect factual information. Five questions will help ensure that you are using deductive logic appropriately.

1. Do I have my facts straight?
2. Is my basic premise(s) connected to facts?
3. Is the syllogism logically derived?
4. Are the inferences valid?
5. Is my conclusion logical?

Whether you use factual knowledge or observation you must use logic. The five questions above should be asked as you make decisions daily. Perhaps this Reminder will be useful.

Reminder
Logical thinking is better than aspirin; it prevents headaches.

REASONING ROADBLOCKS

You probably reason quite well. The vagaries of high-stakes decisions, however, push your mental faculties to the limit. In addition, personality factors that surface under stress serve as reasoning roadblocks. These roadblocks come in various shapes, forms, and types. What is common about them is that they impede your ability to process information and effectively use deductive and inductive logic. Thus, they limit your ability to solve problems and make good judgment calls. Information omission, information block, information overload, information drift, loose logic, connection failure, hot buttons, and false and fuzzy facts are reasoning roadblocks. But each can be removed and replaced by new patterns of thinking. Next is an explanation of each with suggestions for removal.

INFORMATION OMISSION

Information omission is the failure to include facts or ideas that impact the issue or problem. Failure to provide your brain the information it needs is worse than asking a chef to cook a fine meal without the necessary ingredients. Good reasoning cannot overcome a shortage of information. When pieces of information are omitted, analysis and judgment suffer. If you know there is a wild boar in your path, you choose another route. But without that information, you get chewed up badly. When you fail to collect information or skip a step in the data gathering process, you risk being devoured by wild boars or worse. Three thinking approaches cause us to omit information: mindsets, assumption blindness, and jumping to conclusions.

Mindsets. Mindsets are powerful thought waves that influence the way your mind thinks at a given time. These thought waves hinder or help your performance. The next time you hear an Olympic athlete discussing performance, listen for mindset. Drop us a note if the Olympian's thought waves are negative or defeatest. It is uncommon for world class athletes to have negative mindsets; they and their coaches understand the power of positive thinking. Mindsets affect performance. While it is important that you have positive mindsets, it is even more important that your thought waves be free of preconceived notions about people and ideas. If, for example, you have decided that inexperienced teachers are not effective with disadvantaged students, you will be unable or unwilling to collect and analyze any information to the contrary. This mindset will significantly affect judgment calls related to new teachers and disadvantaged students. You manage mindsets by keeping an open mind and collecting and analyzing information objectively. The following Reminder should keep you aware of its importance.

Reminder
Managing your mindset means being optimistic and keeping an open mind.

Assumption blindness. Assumption blindness occurs when you assume something to be true without supporting evidence: GIGO, Garbage In Garbage Out. If your reasoning is based on a false assumption, the conclusion will be wrong. When thinking about a problem, it pays to build an assumption check into the thinking process. Before you factor an assumption into an equation, simply ask yourself to what extent you know it to be true.

Reminder
Assumption checks pay big dividends: They verify the accuracy of information.

Jumping to conclusions. Jumping to conclusions is arriving at the sum before adding up the numbers. Conclusion jumpers typically suffer from a lack of restraint or emotionitis. If you shoot first and ask questions later, you are likely to kill or injure someone. At best you will scare them and waste ammunition. Most administrators who jump to conclusions tend to be action oriented and somewhat impatient. These are good characteristics for leaders, but if you tend to jump to conclusions, you need to find yourself a coping mechanism to slow you down. One of our best bosses always tamped his pipe when presented with a problem. It was only after he retired that we learned he did not smoke. When you want to gun your motor, what can you do to slow yourself down? This suggestion might help you proceed with caution.

- ◆ Use a 3 X 5 card in the same way one of our favorite bosses used his pipe. Write on a 3 X 5 card "STOP AND THINK." On the back of the card write "WHO, WHEN, WHAT, WHERE, AND HOW." Then write, "DO I HAVE THE INFO?" Place this card in your planner or in another location where you can get at it. Take this card out and review the cues when the stakes are high or when you feel yourself rushing to judgment.

Secretarial Suspicions, the next scenario, provides an opportunity to check for understanding and provide feedback. Read the scenario and answer the "check point" questions.

Secretarial Suspicions

Karen is a new principal at Breakwater Elementary. She has been there less than a year while the building secretary Jane Smith has 16 years tenure at that site. Karen had heard from the previous principal that Jane was technically competent but that she frequently gossiped outside the office. Throughout the year, Karen heard information known only to office staff being repeated by teachers and parents. This information ranged from student discipline to employee conduct. Karen began to suspect a breach of confidentiality in the office. After interviewing a number of staff members, Karen narrowed the information leak to her secretary. She had a conference with Jane and developed a plan of improvement, then implemented the plan. Information continued to be leaked. Karen felt she could no longer work with Jane and requested she be transferred. Several weeks later, the Breakwater night custodian reported to Karen that Jane was seen in the main office after hours. Later that day Karen noticed that a locked box of computer disks was missing from the office. These disks contained confidential student and staff information. She thought about the situation and then concluded Jane had taken the discs. Karen reported the incident to the police, implicating Jane as the primary suspect.

CHECK POINT

1. Do you agree with Karen's conclusion? __ yes __ no
2. What information did Karen omit in reaching her conclusion?
3. Why did she omit the information?

We hope you said "no" or "not yet" to the first question. Karen has no information that supports her conclusion. Karen's *mindset* influenced her reasoning; it caused her to stop seeking information. She made no attempt to determine if there was a reason for Jane to be in the building. Had she checked further, she would have learned that Jane was in the building with the lead teacher picking up materials that Jane had inadvertently left in the office. Karen did not jump to a conclusion; she carefully reviewed the information available. She simply did not have the right information. You may think that we are being unfair, that Karen could not have known that Jane was in the building with the lead teacher. Karen should have asked herself if there was any reason for Jane to be in the building and if anyone knew that she was in the building. Guess what, Karen's secretary knew why Jane was in the building but no one asked her. She did not know that Karen was going to report Jane to the police. What was the end result of Karen's judgment call? The police cleared Jane, but Jane is suing Karen. We hope you remember that good information is a prerequisite of good judgment.

It is easy to omit information; it is typically difficult to gather and is time-consuming. Some crutches may help you include the appropriate information:

♦ When you are making an important judgment call, think of it as squeezing the trigger on a high-powered rifle. Ask yourself, "Am I ready to pull the trigger and risk killing or injuring someone?"

♦ Write down Who?, What?, When?, Where?, and How?. Ask yourself whether you have sufficient information to confidently answer these important questions. If you have the information, proceed. If not, go back and collect the information that was omitted.

INFORMATION BLOCK

Information block is an inability to collect or utilize facts and ideas relevant to the problem or issue. In most cases, mindsets block us from collecting data or from analyzing them. Prejudice, stereotypes, bias, and prejudgment insidiously block out information that disables the reasoning process. Some decision makers block out information because they do not like dealing with ambiguity; they are black and white thinkers. Because uncertainty and ambiguity make them uncomfortable, they collect only that information they can process more easily. Ask yourself if you have the relevant information to solve the problem. Note the key question to determine if you are blocking information.

Key Question: Am I blocking out information that I need in order to reason well?

INFORMATION OVERLOAD (TAKE TWO ASPIRINS)

Information overload is what most of us feel when memos, reports, letters, and faxes overwhelm us. It contributes to what we call *take two aspirins*. When was the last time you looked at your desk or in-basket, closed your office door, sat down, opened your desk drawer, and took two aspirins? You'd better have a large bottle. Unless you use an approach like the one described next, the best way to avoid these headaches is to take another job.

In today's world you need a system for processing large amounts of information when solving a problem. Following is an approach to help you sort, scan, select, and discard information. Examine it and then do the practice activity.

Sort	List all information you might need to make the judgment, and sort it by type.
↓	
Scan	Mentally or physically review the content of each item.
↓	
Select	Place a check mark by the information that you will use and mark any you might need.
↓	
Discard	Put aside the remaining information.

INFORMATION DRIFT

Information drift occurs when decision makers change their thinking on an issue each time a new piece of information is received. Picture a principal pulling off flower petals uttering, "She loves me, she loves me not." Each petal is a judgment call. The reasoning process demands that we integrate and weigh new information in a logical and systematic way. The charting process in Chapter 7 provides a formal and a mental system for eliminating information drift.

LOOSE LOGIC

Loose logic is sloppy thinking; it is an improper use of the syllogism. If you know that tightening discipline will result in happier teachers and higher student absenteeism, and you tighten discipline because it will make the teachers feel better, that is sloppy thinking. Unless you do not care about student absenteeism it is like adding 2 and 2 and getting 5. Making the decision to tighten discipline has *caused* another problem—increased absenteeism. It seems ridiculous that anyone would make such a decision, but it happens frequently. Logic has to be tight. Conclusions must flow from tightly coupled cause-and-effect thinking.

CONNECTION FAILURE

Connection failure occurs when the problem solver is unable to connect the elements in the puzzle. Making judgment calls for complex problems is like sitting at a table developing a schemata for wiring a house. The connections between the various currents must be determined, and in problem solving there are positive and negative wires. After you determine the connections between problem elements and their valence, you have a basic understanding of the cause-and-effect relationship within the problem field and how interactions within the field produce unforeseen results. Some decision makers never seem able to make the necessary connections to make a good judgment call. How frequently do you make a decision and then say, "Why didn't I think of that when I was making that call?" If connecting is something you want to improve upon we recommend mindmapping. An explanation is provided in Chapter 9.

HOT BUTTONS

Hot buttons are triggers in your emotional self that inhibit or impede reasoning. When somebody or something triggers anger or fear, emotion prevails over reason and judgment. When a hot button is hit, it frequently causes people to become blind, deaf, and irrational. Decisions become emotional, not reasoned. A hot button may quickly trigger a red hot reaction. For some, these buttons are hard to reach or produce little heat. It is unrealistic to think that you will be able to go through a stress-filled week and keep your hot buttons intact. You must be ready to exercise self-discipline. Understanding your emotional self and what to do when your button is pushed makes it possible to reason effectively. What are your hot buttons? How do you cope when they are pushed? List below three situations that are most likely to trigger your hot buttons, and identify the causes. Then read and consider approaches for maintaining your objectivity.

Hot Button Situations

1. _____

2. _____

3. _____

As you examine these situations determine the underlying factor that pushes your button. Do unfairness, arrogance, power, put downs, or condescending treatment trip your trigger? Write below the underlying cause of your emotions. If there are several, write them down.

Underlying Cause(s)

1. _____

2. _____

3. _____

Now that you have identified your hot buttons, put up your antenna so that when you are in situations where you are vulnerable you are ready to deal with your emotions. Prepare your coping approaches. Here are two coping approaches that work:

◆ *Buy time.* It is very difficult to reason when your emotions are not under your control. When your students are having problems controlling their emotions, you often provide them an opportunity for a time-out. We use an old adage to help us, "When you see red, think red." And red means stop! You simply must discipline yourself to step away from the problem-solving process when you do not have your emotions under control. If you are under the gun to decide quickly, step away anyway; disengaging is always productive.

♦ *Go to the balcony.* Remove your emotional self from the situation. Imagine that you are in a theater and that you are in the balcony watching yourself struggle with your emotions. From your box look down on the issue as if you were a critic, and decide what the actor should do next.

FALSE AND FUZZY FACTS

Facts are to reasoning as air is to humans; we depend on them to function. Incorrect facts result in incorrect judgments. Because interpretation of events or occurrences are filtered through imperfect data gathering mechanisms, bias, prejudice, emotion, and other filters, they create false or fuzzy facts. Facts must be as correct as we can make them. Following are some specific fact-finding suggestions:

♦ Do your best to verify facts in an objective way. Ask other people, examine other data to see if they are parallel, and revisit the source.

♦ Consider the source. Check the reliability and expertise of those providing facts.

♦ Juggle facts to determine if they are internally consistent or if they are contradictory. Follow up or discard isolated facts that do not fit.

♦ Determine if a fact makes sense to you. If it does not, follow up on it to determine its validity or accuracy.

Let us consider a practice case. Read the scenario, and give Winona some advice.

Winona - A Practice Case

Winona is in her second year as principal at Independent In-

termediate School. Independent Intermediate is a fairly typical school with fair test scores and decent facilities. The school had tremendous potential but the previous principal had "retired on the job." Winona was a risktaker. She had been raised by two hard-working parents who believed in the value of work and gave 110% both at home and on their jobs. Winona is intolerant of teachers who do not measure up to her standards. Winona had a vision of what needed to happen at Independent and was enthusiastic in her beliefs. During her first year as principal, she implemented many new programs. Winona feels the school is moving and that she is making progress. She thinks the staff is generally enthusiastic about these ideas. Many staff members put in long hours at implementing these new programs because they liked this spunky principal with the bright ideas. While some veteran staff members are of the belief that Winona and her ideas would be gone before they would be, most staff supported the progress their school was making.

Year number two began smoothly. The staff returned with a renewed enthusiasm and energy. Winona doled out additional responsibilities and new initiatives. Several staff members began to complain about how these new ideas impacted their work load. They questioned Winona's competence, saying she is not focused, she does not involve them prior to implementing an innovation, and they receive little feedback about their progress.

The teachers' association representative met with Winona to share these concerns. The concern spread throughout the school. Soon thereafter, a special faculty meeting was called by some of the staff and Winona has been "requested" to attend. Winona is angry. How could her staff call her on the carpet? She was giving 110% to Independent Intermediate. The meeting is to be held in three days. Winona thinks she may cancel the meeting. She is very frustrated. At the last minute, Winona places a call to a colleague.

If you were Winona 's colleague, what advice would you give Winona? What is your rationale for giving her this advice?

CHECK POINTS

First, tell her not to cancel the meeting. While she is too angry and frustrated to make a good judgment call, she does have time to cool off. There is no pressing need to respond. Suggest to her that she identify why she is frustrated and angry so that she can deal with her emotions. It is quite understandable that she would be frustrated; she has worked hard and was feeling good about how things were going. Get Winona to think about her objective and how change threatens others. Help her to consider the importance of relationships with faculty and the consequences of a shoot-out. Ask her to consider strategies for getting these folks on her side. If none of this helps, tell her to cancel the meeting and go to Tibet; some time with the Dali Llama might help.

KEY BEHAVIORS

DO . . .

+ use experience and reasoning to solve problems.
+ apply formal logic to reach conclusions: premises - syllogism - inference - conclusion.
+ collect information from all sources: phone calls, conversations, etc.
+ keep an open mind, and avoid mindsets.
+ check your assumptions; ask yourself what you know to be true.
+ think more and talk less when gathering information.
+ sort information by its type, select what is relevant, and discard the rest.
+ ask yourself what pieces are missing from this problem puzzle and collect information.

DON'T . . .

- accept generalizations that are not applicable to a situation.

- block out information that needs to be processed.
- be in too much of a hurry to collect needed information.
- let your hot buttons start a fire.
- drift from one conclusion to another as you analyze information.
- discard relevant information before solving a problem.

FOR REFLECTION

Take a few moments to reflect on the reasoning roadblocks. Review the roadblocks and respond to these questions and activities.

♦ Are there any specific roadblocks that you need to overcome to improve your reasoning?

♦ What roadblocks will you reduce or remove? Write a goal and a plan to reduce or eliminate each roadblock.

♦ Develop a method to monitor and assess progress toward your goal.

5

PROBLEM IDENTIFICATION AND ANALYSIS: SCANNING, SCREENING, FOCUSING, AND MAPPING

To see the end from the beginning is not generally given to human kind. —George Rogers

A school leader, like a campaign manager in a hotly contested election, must quickly take stock of the situation and determine the strategy and tactics that lead to victory. All that is missing in the principalship is bare knuckles and backrooms. Success in politics, war, and most complex human endeavors hinges on your ability to identify a problem and break it down so that you can understand it and make decisions. This chapter describes the scanning, screening, focusing, and mapping (SSFM) model, encompassing four tactics that should be in your arsenal. *Problem scanning* (S) will help you recognize problems, while *problem screening* (S) saves time and enables you to focus your attention on the most important problems. *Problem focusing* (F) helps you to zero in on a problem and give it needed attention. *Problem mapping* (M) is a scheme for analyzing the problem by identifying the key features and determining how these features are connected (Figure 5.1). Description of these tactics is followed by an application to a typical school problem.

FIGURE 5.1 SSFM MODEL

Scanning	Monitor environment to recognize problems.
Screening	Filter problem to determine problem priority.
Focusing	Hone in on problem with intensity.
Mapping	Break problem down to determine connection between problem elements.

PROBLEM SCANNING

Let's begin with an important reminder.

Reminder
A problem not recognized is a battle lost.

The best problem solvers are like meteorologists; they constantly scan the environment and check the currents to spot problems on the horizon and in their early stages. Checking the weather is a great American routine. Most of us routinely check the morning paper, the late night report, and the night and morning sky. Makes sense; it is not just Boy Scouts who like to be prepared. Do you believe in the following Advisory?

Advisory: Find problems before they find you.

Problem scanning is not difficult. Set up your radar and sweep the environment. Sweeps include the teachers' lounge, the halls, the community, your office, the newsmedia, memoranda, reports, and anywhere or anything else where people communicate, discuss, or engage in activities that are directly or indirectly related to schooling. While you are more likely to pick up problems related to day-to-day activities, you must also work hard to identify less visible problems. Your radar has three parts: eyes, ears, and mouth. The eyes watch, the ears listen, and the mouth questions. Verbal cues come directly through complaints or are coded through softer words and expressions that reflect concern, frustration, anger, and the like. Nonverbal signs are subtle but powerful: frowns, voice tone, and other body language. The eyes pick up other overt and subtle signs such as arguments and groups of people gathering. The trick is to develop problem scanning to the extent that it becomes a sixth sense; your radar picks up problem cues and alerts you instantly.

PROBLEM SCREENING

When the radar sends a signal back to home base, it simply tells home base that there is something out there and gives it some sense of how to respond. Problem screening enables you to determine whether to make a judgment call or discard or defer it. Six screens enable you to determine if it is your problem, if you have sufficient information to solve it, and the urgency, importance, and timeliness of the problem. These include: jurisdiction, adequacy of information, urgency, importance, timing, and readiness.

JURISDICTION

Effective problem solvers always ask: WHOSE PROBLEM IS IT? Here is a bit of advice that may change your life:

Advisory: If it is not your problem, get rid of it!

If you want to save time and reduce stress, learn how to delegate problems upstream and downstream. Many problems have been messed up or solved by the wrong person. To what extent do you spend much of your day solving others' problems? Do you have faculty members who are willing to let you solve their problems? Do faculty members actively recruit you to be head problem solver? Here is something to help save time and empower staff. Simply take a 3X5 card and write these words on it: "IS THIS MY PROBLEM?" Decide where you will place the card so that you will be constantly reminded of the need to have the right people solving the right problems.

ADEQUACY OF INFORMATION

You cannot determine the urgency or importance of the problem without information. Here is another advisory.

Advisory: Always ask, "Do I have sufficient information to determine the urgency and importance of the problem?"

If not, do not decide. As you move through the problem solving model keep asking yourself if you have sufficient information.

IMPORTANCE AND URGENCY

Every decision is like surgery. Operating on the problem carries with it the risk of shock. Good surgeons do not operate unless surgery is needed to maintain or improve the health of the patient. Sometimes they wait and see if the condition of the patient changes. Understanding the seriousness of a problem and its urgency are fundamental to success. You must determine its importance and urgency. Importance and urgency are independent of each other. A decision about staffing may be important but not urgent because it has a 12-month timeline. A decision about supervision in the lunchroom may not be terribly important but urgent because failure to respond will create a significant problem this noon. The Problem Management Matrix (Figure 5.2) is a modification of a matrix developed by Stephen Covey (1989). It has four quadrants to help you determine the importance and urgency of a decision. Problem-related choices fit into one of four quadrants. As you examine the matrix, think about how you solve problems and how you spend your time.

The four quadrants are represented by four interesting animals. Read the summaries and categorize problems as Sharks, Elephants, Coyotes, and Mice.

FIGURE 5.2 THE PROBLEM MANAGEMENT MATRIX

	Urgent	Not Urgent
Important	**I** Crisis Big values-pressing Important relationships Deadline driven problems	**II** Vision, goals, plans School improvement Program implementation Culture
Not Important	**III** Minor discipline Minor complaints Minor messes Minor conflicts	**IV** Rumors Irrelevant mail Some phone calls Administrivia

Quadrant I. Urgent and Important. These problems are **Sharks**. They require your attention right now. You have to deal with them very quickly and well or you will be history. But you cannot panic, you still must use good judgment or these and other sharks will get you.

Quadrant II. Important but Not Urgent. These problems are **Elephants**. They will trample you to death if you let them, but you have time to prepare, get out in front of them, and turn them around. It is not easy to keep the elephants in sight when the sharks are circling. If you forget the elephants, their sheer weight will eventually overwhelm you.

Quadrant III. Urgent but not Important. They are **Coyotes**. Coyotes circle and snap at you. Individually they are not very dangerous, but if there are enough of them they will eventually eat you alive. Occasionally, one coyote gets meaner and more dangerous than others; keep your guard up.

Quadrant IV. Neither Important nor Urgent. These **Mice** are annoying and irritating. They are not easy to catch, and there are many of them. The most important judgment call you make daily is to ignore, delegate, or spend very little time on the mice. Do be careful, though. If you completely ignore them they will multiply and overrun your office.

The matrix provides a practical guide for dealing with problems. When the Sharks are circling, deal with them first or they will destroy you. Give the Elephants thinking time. Keep your eyes (and mind) on the Coyotes. Complaints, discipline, meetings, minor conflicts, and the like need to be dealt with despite the limited payoff. You have to be very disciplined to ignore the Mice; they are irritating. They sometimes lure you in because they are relatively easy to deal with and make you feel good.

TIMING

Is now the time? This is a biggie. Far too many administrators implemented an otherwise good alternative only to find that the perceptions or emotions of the moment made it a very bad choice. These perceptions are typically affected by events and environmental factors. A decision to loosen up on discipline is perilous, if it follows a riot or gang incident. During hard economic times, a problem related to money often becomes more important.

READINESS

You must be mentally and emotionally ready to solve the problem. If you are angry, distracted, anxious, or for any other reason not ready to objectively analyze the problem, get ready quick or wait for a better time. If it is urgent and you are not ready, stall as long as you can.

4D PROBLEM SCREEN

The 4D Problem Screening Guide (Figure 5.3) uses the six screens as a guide in making a very big judgment call that you consciously or unconsciously make each time you recognize a problem. That judgment call revolves around whether to Discard, Defer, Decide, or Diagnose/Decide. Jurisdiction, urgency, importance, timing, adequacy of information, and readiness are the criteria you use in determining whether to move or wait. If it is not your problem or is unimportant, discard it. If it is your problem and it is important, but not urgent, and the timing is bad or you do not have adequate information or you are not ready, defer it. If it is your problem, is important and urgent, the timing is appropriate, and you have adequate information and are ready, decide. If you are not ready because you have not thought through the problem sufficiently or are not emotionally ready, diagnose/decide.

FOCUSING

Did you ever observe Jack Nicklaus stalking a putt? Do you remember the concentration of Mary Lou Retton before she hit a "10" and won the Olympic gold? What do Goren, Spassky, Michael Johnson, three champions in bridge, chess, and track, all have in common? Obviously, all have talent and drive. What places these champions on a higher plane than their talented competition is their incredible ability to focus, to totally

FIGURE 5.3 THE 4D PROBLEM SCREENING GUIDE

Screen	Key Question
Jurisdiction	Is it my problem?
Adequacy of Information	Do I have sufficient information?
Urgency	How urgent is it?
Importance	How important is it?
Timing	Is now the time?
Readiness	Am I emotionally ready?
Problem Choices	
Discard	Do not deal with problem.
Defer	Address problem at a later time.
Decide	Make judgment call.
Diagnose/Decide	Collect and analyze information, then decide.

concentrate on the task at hand. The most successful people have the ability to block out distractions to focus on the goal and do what needs to be done to reach that goal. Alan Alda said it best: "When I am trying to solve a problem or learn something, I do tend to get obsessed with it. But I find I can only accomplish what I want to accomplish by a process of total absorption." Alda has it right. When you solve a problem, you must become totally absorbed and bring all of your skill and energy to bear on the problem. Here is a self-test. Check yourself out.

FOCUSING SELF-TEST

To what extent do you focus when solving problems? Take a few moments to analyze your behavior when solving problems by responding to the following questions.

1. You are supervising the cafeteria during the lunch shift. A teacher approaches you about a theft that has just occurred in his classroom. What do you do?

2. You are in your office conducting a productive conversation with a mentor teacher. Your secretary interrupts you to inform you that there is an irate parent on the phone who demands to speak with you immediately. What do you do?

3. While chatting with a colleague on the phone, you overhear a student messenger report that the secretary thinks one of the students has broken a leg. You know the PE teachers have been teaching a unit on field hockey and there have been several minor accidents so far this year. A district nurse is in your building today. What do you do next?

The correct answer to all three questions is focus. Tune out, and tune in. Tune out other mice, sharks, elephants, and coyotes that are nipping at you, and tune in to the immediate problem. You cannot think about two problems at once; your brain is incapable of such a feat. Clear from your mind anything that impedes your ability to see, hear, think, or feel your way to the problem solution. The next Reminder says it all.

Reminder
You cannot do anything about the problem you just had or may have; kill this one, and you have done your job.

Focusing is not a passive activity. Have you ever watched a tiger stalk another animal? It zeroes in every bit of its attention on its prey; it is oblivious to everything around it. Successful coaches have very specific ways of focusing. They shield from view anything that can distract them from focusing on a specific area or player. That is what you must do when you focus on a problem in your school. You must learn how to do it, and do it well. Consider some specific suggestions to sharpen your focusing technique:

1. When you are solving a problem of importance clear your mind, and write down the problem. Remind yourself that you can only focus on one thing at a time. Now, think **FOCUS** and **INTENSITY**.

2. Visualize the problem or something directly related to the problem. Think only about it. Record problem details on a pad. Then, think more deeply about the problem, add details, and visualize the connections among problem elements.

3. Think about the impact of the problem on you and others in your school.

4. Think of a worst case and best case scenario that can result from your effort to solve the problem.

PROBLEM MAPPING

Problem mapping is a systematic way to break down a problem so that it can be analyzed effectively. Problem factors are unknown, disconnected fragments until specifically identified and connected. The most effective way to identify key factors and determine connections is to collect information that provides insight into what occurred and how various problem elements are connected. Figure 5.4 lists nine problem mapping elements and the big questions that must be answered to properly analyze the problem. We then provide a scenario to use the mapping elements to map a real problem.

A problem map provides some insight into what makes problem analysis challenging. Answering the big questions is no easy task. These elements are elusive, complex, and rapidly changing. The good news is that the more you specifically target elements and systematically ask questions, the more effective your problem solving. A Matter of Discipline provides an opportunity to map a fairly typical problem. Read the problem, and map it. Then compare your map with the one we provide to see if you agree with our application of map elements.

A Matter of Discipline
Your school is located in a neighborhood that has deteriorated significantly during your four years as a principal at Piney

FIGURE 5.4 PROBLEM MAPPING GUIDE

Problem Elements	Big Questions
People	Who is involved and in what way?
Actions/Events	What actions and/or events occurred?
Sequence	What was the order or sequence of actions and events?
Timing	When did actions/events occur, and when did people do whatever they did?
Perceptions	How do individuals and groups view the matter?
Assumptions, Beliefs	What assumptions, beliefs, values, and attitudes have impact?
Cause/Effect	What are the causes-effect relationships, and why did certain events and actions cause problems?
Key Factors	What are the key factors to be considered in better understanding the problem?
Relationships	What are the relationships among key factors, people, perceptions, actions, events, time, sequence, and cause and effect?

Middle School. More than 90% of your students are now on free and reduced lunch, and there is considerable gang activity around the school. It has been an interesting four years. Since becoming the principal, you have revamped a student management system that once relied heavily on rules and punishment. The staff's answer to most student problems was to demand suspension or expulsion. An alarming percentage of Piney students receive failing grades; reading and math test scores are abysmal. Your PTA is not very active, but many parents come to school to voice their concerns and frustrations about the manner in which their kids are being treated by teachers.

You have made some efforts to turn this thing around, but a veteran faculty plays the blame game and uses their master contract as a weapon. While you have some new teachers who support change, many of the faculty see rules, strong discipline, and punishment as the only way to maintain control of their classrooms and the school. Your approach to date has been to implement staff development to improve classroom teaching and provide students a more supportive atmosphere. Typically, when considering change, you talk to supportive faculty members, enlist their support, and then do whatever you think will be the best approach for the kids.

You recently did just that with Project Achieve, an approach that requires teachers to receive training and then teach students social skills. You were going to put implementation of Project Achieve up for a vote, but the faculty was angry about a number of things and probably would have voted it down. Because of a significant financial commitment to Project Achieve, you decided to implement it. On your desk is a letter signed by the teacher union representative and four other teachers who are seen as leaders by the faculty.

❖ ❖ ❖ ❖

Dear Principal,

This faculty is thoroughly frustrated with the lack of leadership in this school. During the four years that you have been principal, you have relaxed discipline and grading standards to the point that we are no longer able to control student behavior or have reasonable expectations for them.

While we agree that these students need attention and understanding, we cannot act as parent/guardian and school psychologist for every student who has problems. We also believe that allowing disruptive children to stay in school and socially promoting them is unfair to them and to the community at large. You should also know that this faculty will no longer tolerate the imposition of programs and approaches that are unsound. In addition to the harm that they bring to children, they are in violation of the district's site-based management policy and the state's school improvement statutes. This latest effort (Project Achieve) will waste valuable time on nonacademic matters. It is clearly inappropriate and will not be tolerated.

We strongly recommend that you stop this project immediately and that you also reinstitute the discipline code and consequences that you have changed over the past four years. If you fail to do so, we will ask each staff member to file a grievance and will also report to central administration our lack of confidence in this administration.

Sincerely,

Arthur K.
Todd R.
Sally K.
Lila A.

A MATTER OF DISCIPLINE - PROBLEM MAPPING

Let us identify the problem elements in *A Matter of Discipline* and then analyze them to solve the problem.

People: Who is involved and in what way? The importance of a problem, its urgency, and its solution are frequently a function of who is involved or will be affected by the action or events. Some call this politics. We call it reality. Whatever it is called, it is important. If you disagree, try ignoring your board president or superintendent. The parents are a factor in this problem; many have come to school to express concern. The scenario provides insufficient information about the parents. Obviously students are involved; the problem has implications for the student body. The staff is involved. Do you wish you had more information about how other staff members were reacting to this issue? In the real world you would. The four teachers who signed the letter are very involved and are leaders. The principal is the other key person in this problem. His or her beliefs, values, preferences, and orientation to the problem must be factored into the problem analysis. You must take stock—of yourself—when you analyze a problem. The other key people not mentioned in the scenario are central office and community. Their involvement is implicit; they will probably become aware of this problem and react to the principal's decision.

Action/Events: What actions and/or events occurred? Problems are always preceded by action or events. It is important to determine what led to the problem as quickly as possible. Provided is a list of related actions and events:

- Students received failing grades.
- Parents came to school and complained about student failure.
- Principal initiated activities to make the school more student-oriented. This includes attempts to be more supportive of students, implementation of approaches to student discipline that are less punitive than those previously employed, plus implementation of a project to improve the school.
- Staff reacted by demanding suspension or expulsion.
- Staff development provided to teachers.
- Principal talked to supportive teachers.
- Project Achieve initiated.
- Four teachers and teacher union representative write letter expressing dissatisfaction and threatening action against the principal.

Sequence: What was the order of the action or events? The sequence of events or actions is the source for determining cause and effect. Problems are usually a result of a sequence of activities. The list of actions/events just presented have been written in the sequence in which they occurred.

Timing: When did things occur, and to what extent does the timing of action/events influence the problem and alternative solutions? The information given provides limited help to analyze timing. Obviously the gang activity has an impact here; the faculty may be expecting more discipline and security measures. Parents have complained about how their kids are being treated so they may be expecting support from the principal.

Perceptions: How do individuals and groups view the problem? Perceptions are more powerful than actions or events; how we perceive actions and events creates our reality. Perceptions are influenced by a number of factors. History, culture, mindsets, beliefs, values, and other factors color our view of events and actions. For example, we are more likely to view an action or event that once caused us pain in a different light than one that provided significant pleasure. It is important to do your very best to determine people's perceptions.

It is apparent that some parents see the school or teachers as the problem. The attitudes of the four teachers are quite clear, but we do not know why they perceived the principal's actions as they did nor do we know how other teachers, or how parents, central office, or community members view the problem. More information is needed.

Assumptions, Beliefs, Values, and Attitudes: What assumptions, beliefs, values, and attitudes have an impact? Assumptions, beliefs, values, and attitudes impact actions and perceptions of others' actions. The scenario does not tell us much about the beliefs, values, attitudes, and assumptions of the parents or staff. It is possible that the four teacher leaders believe in involvement and are upset because they think this is top down. You should know the beliefs, values, attitudes, and assumptions within your school, district, and community and include them in mapping the problem. Little information has been provided here.

Cause/Effects: What are the cause and effect relationships within the problem? To effectively analyze a problem, you must be able to determine cause and effect. It appears that teacher behavior has elicited a negative reaction from parents. The known effects of the principal's initiation of a student management system are teacher dissatisfaction. We are not sure of the effects of the staff development. Initiation of Project Achieve resulted in the letter from the four teachers and the rep.

Key Factors: What are the key factors to be considered in analyzing the problem? When you think of the number of factors in each of the elements, it is easy to understand why problem solving is so challenging; the number of factors to consider can be staggering. You have to identify the most significant aspects of the problem. To determine these factors, you must understand cause and effect and the political, economic, social, and psychological environment in which you work. That knowledge helps you to weigh and identify those factors that are most important. In this case, and in many problems, a number of key factors are found in the actions, whereas others are inferred from examining the information and making certain assumptions:

- Kids (low SES) are failing—need for change.
- Principal there for four years.
- Issues involve student discipline.
- Principal trying to change things—programs, staff development, etc.
- Teachers asked to teach social skills.
- Many staff resisting.
- New teachers may be supportive.
- Union and contract a factor mitigating change.
- Parents not happy about school and teachers.
- Teacher leaders are upset.
- Teachers threatening grievances and to go to central office.
- Financial commitment to project has been made.

Relationships: What are the relationships between key factors, people, perceptions, actions, events, time, sequence, and cause and effect? The relationships in this case are classic. Teachers' reaction to the perceived inappropriate behavior of low SES children leads to parent dissatisfaction. Student failure, parent reaction, and the principal's need to address these problems led to initiation of the project.

The Bottom Line. The principal should neither discard this problem nor simply defer it. The principal, however, has not sufficiently diagnosed or analyzed the problem to make a decision. It is the principal's problem but there is insufficient information to make a judgment. The problem is important and somewhat urgent. It involves key people and is potentially dangerous. More information must be collected and weighed carefully. To make a definitive call to action now would be a mistake; diagnose and decide is the appropriate choice.

KEY BEHAVIORS

Do . . .

+ scan the environment to find problems before they find you.
+ screen problem to determine priority.
+ focus on problem with attention and intensity.
+ map problem to identify pieces and connections.
+ ask, Is it my problem?
+ ask, Is now the time?
+ ask, Do I have sufficient information?
+ ask, Am I ready to solve this problem?
+ ask, Is this a Shark, Elephant, Coyote, or Mouse?
+ Discard, Defer, Decide, or Diagnose and then Decide.
+ create a Problem Map template on your computer and in your head.

+ use the map and the Big Questions next time you solve a problem.
+ tape the Big Questions to your think area.

Don't . . .

- solve others' problems.
- solve problems without a system.

For Reflection

♦ Write down how you will make the SSFM Model a part of your daily operating procedure.

♦ Think about how you will make the six screens part of your daily operating procedure.

♦ What are you going to do to move out of Quadrants 3 and 4 and into Quadrant 2?

♦ Take a few moments and make a few notes as to how you can use problem mapping to make better judgment calls.

6

BEST ALTERNATIVES

*The creative process does not end with a good idea; it
starts with one. Creative ideas are just the first step in a long process
of bringing thoughts into reality.—Alex Osborn*

Good decisions flow from good alternatives. Quality counts when generating alternatives to solve a challenging school problem. This Reminder puts it in the proper perspective:

Reminder
*You can never make a judgment call better than the quality of
the alternatives from which you choose.*

There are, however, no prepackaged lists of dynamite alternatives for the weird, wonderful, and unique problems you encounter daily. Knowledge and creativity are your best tools for generating the best alternatives, those that give you the best outcome. This chapter will help you crank up your creativity. First, there is a self-check. We then discuss creative thinking and provide suggestions for unlocking ideas. We wrap up the chapter with some practical suggestions for cranking up creativity.

SEEKING ALTERNATIVES

When the alternatives to solve a problem are limited, it makes sense to simply evaluate the alternatives and choose one or more that will give you the best outcome. Most problems, however, have no fixed set of alternatives; you must develop them. That is the basis of the next Reminder:

Reminder
The quality of alternatives is only limited by our capacity to develop them.

Most effective problem solvers generate alternatives of significantly higher quality than their less effective colleagues because they are able to avoid the "Limited Choice Trap." When people get caught in the limited choice trap, they grab an "experience alternative," something that worked in the past. Time constraints, mindsets, old paradigms, and the need for safety tend to cause them to hold onto old ways. Do you get caught in the Limited Choice Trap? Check yourself out.

Limited Choice Trap Quiz
Read each statement below. Check the response column that best describes you and your problem-solving tendency.

	Not Like Me	Somewhat Like Me	Like Me
1. When discussing problems, I tend to rely on successful solutions used in my last school or assignment.	___	___	___
2. When resolving problems, I spend more time selecting the solution than generating ideas.	___	___	___
3. I rarely spend time brainstorming ideas.	___	___	___
4. I mentally reject ideas that appear risky.	___	___	___
5. I do not feel I have time to spend brainstorming solutions.	___	___	___
6. I tend to select safe solutions.	___	___	___

7. I rely on others to generate
solutions. ___ ___ ___

8. I am not a risk taker. ___ ___ ___

If you checked "like me" or "somewhat like me" for five or more statements, it is very easy for you to become stuck in the Limited Choice Trap. You may not be finding time to generate solutions or are not thinking creatively.

CREATIVE THINKING

What are the natural attributes of creative thinkers? Brookfield (1989) identified commonalties of creative thinkers. Check the column that best describes you.

Creative Thinking Check-Up

	Not Like Me	Somewhat Like Me	Like Me
1. Reject standardized formats for problem solving.	___	___	___
2. Wide interests in education and related fields.	___	___	___
3. Take multiple perspectives on a problem.	___	___	___
4. View the world as messy and ever changing.	___	___	___
5. Frequently use trial and error to experiment with alternatives.	___	___	___
6. Future-oriented and embrace change.	___	___	___
7. Self-confident and trust judgment.	___	___	___

If you answered "like me" or "somewhat like me" to most of

these questions, you will probably read the remainder of this chapter because of your broad interests. If these characteristics do not describe you, do not get frustrated or close the book; creative thinkers are rare. So are world class athletes. But it is probably easier for you to become a creative thinker than a world class athlete. Developing creative thinking is achievable. Creative thinkers have been studied by cognitive psychologists. Most fit under one of five classifications: *field-independent, lateral, holistic, divergent, and syllabus-free.* Examine these types and determine the classification in which you have the greatest strength.

Field-Independent: How good are you at taking ideas and information and using them to create new ideas? If you are an idea person, you may be a field-independent thinker. Field independent thinkers have a highly developed capacity for cognitive restructuring, for taking a field of cognitive information that has been structured to produce one set of concepts and restructuring it to produce others. They run various options through their head until a flash of insight sparks a new alternative. Check the column that best describes you.

Not Like me   Like Me

Divergent: When you are searching for a solution, do you tend to follow a preset routine and come up with the answer? If you follow a preset routine you are probably not a divergent thinker. Divergent thinkers often do not follow a predefined, standardized format when problem solving. They tend to see problems as situational and enjoy brainstorming creative solutions. They especially enjoy unique and open problems because these problems provide them an opportunity to do what comes naturally (to them), think in a different way.

Not Like me   Like Me

Lateral: Do you tend to get "stuck" on an idea and have trouble moving away from it? Is it hard for you to jump from one idea to another? Are you more comfortable dealing with one idea? Are you adept at moving across topics and scanning or inventing others? Do you get excited when you have the opportunity to brainstorm and enjoy developing new ideas? If this describes you, you are a lateral thinker, your mind roams across ideas always thinking of possibilities.

Not Like me   Like Me

_____

Holistic: Raise your hand if you are good at seeing the big picture. In any principals' meeting where that directive is given, far more hands are raised than should be. Most of us find it much easier to deal with pieces. Most minds find it difficult to think about people, action, events, and situational factors within the problem. The ability to see the people, actions, events, time, and sequence in the problem field and to determine how these are connected describes the holistic thinker.

Not Like me   Like Me

_____

Syllabus-free: Do you enjoy future-oriented problem solving? Do you get a kick out of sitting in a room with others brainstorming what might be done in the future even though it has no practical application in your school or district? Do you like to mess around with scenarios and build models? If you are inclined to answer "yes" to most or all of these questions, you are a syllabus-free thinker. You do not want to be hampered by a curriculum; you would rather solve problems where interests and the future are most important.

Not Like me   Like Me

_____

STRENGTHEN YOUR CREATIVE THINKING

Let us build on your strength. Identify the creative thinking type(s) that is most like you, and use the extension strategy to build on that strength.

Thinking Type	Extension Strategy
Field-Independent	Set aside time to use the information you have to create new ideas. Try mindmapping, described in Chapter 9.
Divergent	You enjoy and are effective at brainstorming. Put yourself in situations where you can free-think about unique problems.
Lateral	See yourself as a scanner, and let your brain scan all the ideas that are within its beam. Allow time for scanning.
Holistic	Use mindmapping and other approaches that enable you to see the big picture. Then use your natural tendency to create by connecting pieces in the picture.
Syllabus-free	You have the ability to make something out of nothing, to dream and to create a vision. Put yourself in situations where you can dream and create.

Unlocking Possibility Thinking

The biggest barrier to creative thinking is "mindyapping," inner voices telling you things that lock you out of possibilities. Every living, breathing individual with a principal's certificate hears inner voices. These voices can limit you if you let them. You must learn to quiet inner voices that inhibit creativity. Despite the numerous mindlocks that hinder creativity, mind-opening keys can unlock your creative talents.

The Right Answer. How many right answers are there on a multiple choice test? In this country we learn that the payoff comes from identifying the right answer. Our businesses reinforce being right. We practice it in our daily lives. Most of us spend a good portion of our lives learning and practicing how to do the right thing. Your inner voice is hollering, "Evaluate and choose the right answer."

Mind-Opening Key - Put this sign in your daily planner: <u>Nothing is more dangerous than an idea when it is the only one you have.</u> Ask your inner voice to remind you that there are very few right answers in the school business.

That's Not Logical. Applying the rules of logic early in the thinking process locks you out of breakthrough ideas. Your inner voice is chanting, "That is not logical. What are the facts? It does not add up!"

Mind-Opening Key - After you have identified and analyzed the problem, have your inner voice whisper, "Create!" Discipline yourself to explore ideas with no limits or evaluation involved. Ask your inner voice to remind you that answers to complex and messy problems often come from daydreaming or brainstorming.

Be Practical. Does your inner voice tell you to be sensible and practical? How loud does it sound? Being practical requires evaluation and judgment. Your creativity assassin wears a Black Hat; judgment is an idea killer. It is a proven fact that many dumb ideas work if they survive.

Mind-Opening Key - Put your Green Hat on and grow some ideas. Let your brain maximize its potential. We promise not to tell anyone about your silly ideas if you will let us use them. Remember, you can always put on your Black Hat, but you cannot wear a Black Hat and a Green Hat at the same time. Tell your inner voice to remind you that great ideas are practical because they work.

To Err Is Wrong. Does your inner voice tell you that it is better to be safe than sorry? While you obviously should not take risks that jeopardize students, it is important to realize that the safety and security that comes with staying "inside the box" has not been giving us the desired results.

> *Mind-Opening Key* - As you begin thinking about ideas or problem solutions, ask yourself two questions, "What is the worst thing that could happen if I really come up with a new idea?" Then ask, "What is the best thing that could happen?" If that does not convince you, keep on getting what you always got. Ask your inner voice to remind you that if you are trying new and innovative ways to solve problems, you will make a few mistakes, but you will also get better results.

IDEA CREATION

You were born creative. Do not cheat yourself. The creativity process has distinct stages that enable you to think creatively. If you choose to be the best you can be, your creativity needs to be nurtured. Examine the stages and determine how to make them work for you.

Stage I - Preparation. You cannot drink from an empty bucket, nor can you create from an empty head. Possibility thinking requires a broad knowledge or information base. Creativity flows from a broad interest base as well. Fill your mind with information directly and indirectly related to the problem. Learn the technical side of your work, but do not forget to learn life's lessons. Understanding the world around you is a prerequisite for making good judgment calls. A supply of good books is a great help.

- ◆ Read about life and your work.
- ◆ Never miss a chance to add to your knowledge base through new experiences such as travel, seminars.
- ◆ Listen to others' opinions about life and work.
- ◆ Collect as much information about the problem as you can.

Stage II - Incubation. Find your most productive thinking time, and use it to create alternatives. Think of your past experiences. What times have been most productive? Align your schedule to find time to use your mind most productively.

♦ Schedule down time so you can think.

♦ Schedule one two-hour period for thinking per week.

♦ Mull over important problems.

Stage III - Illumination. Sudden bursts of knowledge and ideas invariably come after your conscious mind has ceased work on a problem. Your subconscious mind then massages and connects concepts and AHA! The answer frequently dawns, hits you, when you are completely relaxed doing something such as jogging, showering, or driving your car.

♦ Schedule relaxation into your day and week.

♦ When ideas come, go with the flow.

Stage IV - Implementation. No creative idea is valued until it provides benefits. The final step in solving a practical problem is enlisting the support of other people, locating the necessary resources, and putting the pieces together to reach the objective.

♦ Identify the key people who can make a solution work.

♦ Enlist these key people, and get their support.

♦ Form the egg — Turn the problem over until it has become a complete and understandable whole.

♦ Lay the egg — Drop it from conscious thought, and let your subconscious work on it.

♦ Sit on it — Let your conscious mind rest.

♦ Hatch it — Let the ideas come out.

♦ Crate it—Write it down.

These stages and strategies are important. Creativity does not bubble up from an empty vessel; information and knowledge have to be stored. Ideas have to incubate. Big ideas need more time and deeper reflection. Nobody ever reported having a big idea during a fire drill. The best AHAs! are created when your mind has an opportunity to create a new idea.

PATHS TO CREATIVE IDEAS

When was the last time you needed to be creative and got stuck? It is quite common to find yourself without ideas when you need them the most. There are specific approaches to a path that leads to better ideas. Figure 6.1 shows the path to follow in creating a new idea.

FIGURE 6.1 PATH TO CREATIVE IDEAS

Old Idea ➲ Concept ➲ Provocation ➲ Movement ➲ New Idea

Your thinking begins with whatever idea finds its way into your mind. When an old idea insinuates itself into your thoughts, it is easy for you to grasp it as a concept and to hold onto it. Provocations are attempts to jerk your mind out of the groove of old ideas. De Bono (1990) refered to provocations as PO (Provocative Operation). We will refer to it as a PO to help you to remember it. De Bono provided an example of the power of provocation. During seminars with Xerox in which managers were working on problems with copy machine design and sales, the group became bogged down and could generate few solutions outside those that had not worked before. Then they used a PO. The consultant asked them to think of how associating their nose with copiers could help them to solve their problem. The participants began thinking about and discussing the smell of copying and moved away from the ideas that were taking them nowhere. The consultant used a provocation to get them out of their rut, and new ideas were hatched. A provocation is a deliberately "unreasonable" way to jerk your thinking out of its normal channels. You simply use an outrageous idea that might be used to solve the problem to move you to other ideas that will be productive.

One of the judgment calls your brain continuously makes as it processes information is to ask, "What have we here?" The brain constantly seeks to find, identify, and match appropriate patterns. This activity is somewhat automatic, although you do help the process along. The brain also locates mistakes and gets your thinking back on track. Your brain tells you, for example, that a school with naked teachers might not fit in your community. In traditional brainstorming, you are told to suspend or delay judgment about such ideas because judgment blocks creativity. Telling us what not to do does not rev up creativity. Movement does rev up creativity. Movement is a conscious act of moving to a new idea. Three techniques will help create new ideas.

1. *Extract a Principle*. You are having a difficult time keeping your building clean and you are stuck for alternatives. Think of a PO. Then work at extracting a principle from it. Here is an example.

> *PO: Hire a robot. Although hiring a robot may not make much sense to you, the notion of using a robot may give you new ideas. Robots are seldom sick. They never get angry. They can work for very long periods of time. They follow directions very well. They can repeat routines very well. They do not waste time. (These are the principles you extracted from the PO.) These somewhat far out ideas move you to another idea. Perhaps a better system, not training, would improve building maintenance. Perhaps an efficiency approach could be employed. The PO stimulated the movement to the new idea.*

2. *Moment to Moment*. Trust us on this one. Identify a PO and how it would be put into effect. Then visualize the moment-to-moment happenings. It is like watching a videotape frame by frame. As you watch the frames, you develop some interesting ideas and concepts.

PO: I hired the robot, and the robot immediately began to systematically clean the building. People watched the robot and also began to work at keeping the building cleaner. The robot developed a schedule and procedures that ensured that the cleaning was done efficiently. As I visualize all this, I get ideas as to what we can do now.

3. Positive Effects. This is a very simple movement technique. Identify a PO and the benefits of the PO. Then take the benefit and identify an idea that could produce this benefit.

PO: The robot will result in people taking pride in a clean building. Perhaps if I began a "Pride in D&J Hall" campaign, I could get the same result.

Have you got the idea? Can you use PO to move to possibility thinking? Let us examine how Einstein used it and then try a few PO's. When Einstein was searching for solutions to complex problems, he often asked himself the following question: *What would I see if I were traveling at the speed of light?*

Did Einstein use creative visualization to connect to possible ideas that would solve the problem? That is not why he did it. It was used as a provocation; Einstein used it to disconnect, not connect. He wanted to get out of a rut, so he moved away from his old ideas using a PO. Let us use the process to practice becoming more creative when solving problems. Assume you are working with Mr. Smith who is having problems in his classroom. You want to help him improve his performance and think that a mentor would help. Mentors do not grow on trees, so you need to think creatively to solve your problem. Thus, mentor becomes the "idea" or problem solution on which you are working. It is important that you identify the concept that idea represents. When you thought of a mentor as a solution, you were thinking of a significant helper, one who could observe and coach Smith. Thus, the concept in the creative path is helper. You have been thinking about the various approaches or alternatives that would provide a helper. You identify a few other alternatives, such as partner and peer coach and then run dry. This is when you would use a PO. Take a few minutes, identify a PO to help you solve the problem with Mr. Smith. Write down the PO, apply it to the problem, and note the results.

CREATIVITY CRANKS

There are other things you do to crank up your creative thinking. Examine the activities provided and choose at least one that you will use as a Creativity Crank.

Creative Pause. You are faced with a decision as to what to do about the lack of parent involvement in your school. You have had a tough day and have a lot of things on your mind. You may have generated a list of the things you have done previously and read some materials related to parent involvement. Now is the time for a creative pause. Interrupt your activities or what you are thinking and create. Never make an important decision without employing a creative pause. Seldom act without pausing. Do not stay with a line of thinking without a creative pause; the creative pause is a very useful tool. You are more likely to create a better solution to your parent involvement problem if you take a creative pause.

Green Hat Thinking. Buy yourself a Green Hat and put it in your office. When you need new ideas sit down and put on your Green Hat. When you leave your office, imagine that you will have your Green Hat on all day. Think of vegetation and growth when you are faced with a problem and need to generate new ideas.

Play. Play imagination games. Galileo's telescope was his toy; he played at inventing. Animals stimulate our sense of job and our imagination. As you work with people, do they remind you of an animal or bird? We hope your boss is a teddy bear. Find as many ways as you can to be playful and to imagine things.

Strengthen Your Creative Muscle. Take every opportunity you can to exercise your mind. If you do not, your mind muscles will atrophy and become weak. You must also exercise your mind so that it does not become too tense. Do not think hard for too long or stress will hamper your thinking. Think and then let your mind rest. Try mind bending exercises.

Mental Practice. Rehearsal improves effectiveness. One good way to solve problems and improve your judgments is to mentally practice reaching conclusions and solving problems.

Project Yourself to the End. Whenever you are faced with a problem that demands creativity, develop a vision of the problem as a completed project. Visualize the means you might use to solve the problem and the results.

Use Mind Joggers. Idea checklists are the same as grocery lists; they tell you what needs to be remembered. Take a piece of paper and quickly jot down all the ideas you have that might solve a problem. Examine the list, and jot down some more. You will be able to do so because your mind was jogged.

Be a Searcher. You cannot drink from an empty bucket. Learn about the things that are related to the problems you are tying to solve. Enjoy the quest to learn more and think better.

Be Curious and Question. Searching for what we do not know is a creative act. Ask questions. Here are the key questions: Who? Why? How? What? When? So what? After you have asked all these questions, it helps you to determine what you learned. Ask this question: Well?

Persevere. Creative effort produces results. You must work at it. As Einstein said, "Genius is 1% inspiration and 99% perspiration." You have to strategically obsess on a problem to solve it. Identify your objective. Think about it! Create alternatives! Walk away and forget about it. Think more at Level 2! Hang with it until you are satisfied.

KEY BEHAVIORS

Do . . .

+ practice the rules of brainstorming when generating alternatives.

+ keep a list of all alternatives. If these do not solve your current problem, they may be valuable in the future.

+ use a Provocative Operation to expand your list of alternatives.

+ put this sign in your planner: "Nothing is more dangerous than an idea when it is the only one you have."

+ spend five minutes each day daydreaming.

+ create a Wild Idea Wall and place all your wild ideas there.

+ switch think spots with a friend for a week.

+ give yourself a BRAIN BURST by tasting a new food, listening to alternative music, wearing a new perfume or cologne.

+ develop a quality office library and read it!

+ talk educational or life philosophy with someone with an alternative view.

+ schedule relaxation into your day.

+ identify key people who can help you achieve your idea.

+ enlist their support.

DON'T . . .

- let books, videos, CDs get dusty.

- reject ideas that appear to be risky.

- limit yourself to pet solutions .

- limit yourself to a single solution.

- apply the rules of logic early in the thinking process.

FOR REFLECTION

♦ Write down at least one thing you will do to dream and think that will make you more creative.

♦ Review the section on provocation and decide how you will use provocation to generate alternatives.

♦ Identify the creativity cranks that will enable you to be more creative, and decide when and how to employ them.

7

BEST CHOICE

Ideas are cheap and abundant: What is of value is the effective
placement of those ideas into situations that develop into action.
—*Peter Drucker*

Identify the problem, collect, organize, process, synthesize, analyze, and evaluate information. These are activities in which you engage to make high-stakes judgment calls. Ambiguity, uncertainty, needs, preferences, values, feelings, and attitudes interact with detail complexity. In *The Science of Muddling Through,* Carl Lindblom (1959) pointed out that there are no "right choices" for leaders, that success is often relative. "Messy problems and no-win choices leave little choice but muddling through." The best choice is not perfect; it is most beneficial over the long haul. The process used to make that choice must have order but may not be orderly. This chapter provides a way to sift, sort, and select your way to good decisions. Six questions that provide a framework for achieving the best outcome are accompanied by a brief explanation of their use. These are followed by a description of the two phases of Choice Charting.

BEST CHOICE FRAMEWORK

In determining the best choice, there are six critical questions that must be answered:

1. What is the problem objective(s)?
2. Will it benefit students?
3. What are the benefits and unintended consequences?
4. What are the short- and long-term effects?
5. Is it morally/ethically right?
6. Is it the best choice for this situation at this point in time?

The Problem Objective. If you do not know where you are going, any place will do. If you do not know what you want to accomplish, any outcome is satisfactory. You cannot make good choices without an objective. Stephen Covey (1989) had another way of conceptualizing the need for objectives, "Begin with the end in mind." That end becomes your vision, target, or objective. The importance of the problem objective cannot be overstated. The objective delimits the problem and provides the frame for evaluating the alternatives. Developing and using problem objectives to solve problems is a way of thinking. When a problem appears at your door, phone, or desk, if you will simply ask yourself what outcome(s) you are striving for as a result of solving the problem, you will have the end in mind that will give you the greatest payoff. Ask yourself, "What outcomes do I want and for whom?" When a student is sent to the office for an infraction of your discipline code, you have a problem. After you collect the necessary information and analyze the problem, the question is, "What outcomes do I want and for whom?" I want to change the student's behavior. I want the teacher to feel supported. I want the parent to support the discipline. The alternative you choose to solve the problem is then evaluated in terms of its value or worth in meeting that objective. That is the process you use to get the best results as you solve problems throughout the day.

Benefit to Students. The one constant objective in problem solving at the school level is benefit to students. Many of the choices you make have an indirect effect on students that is difficult to determine. A judgment about student discipline, for example, may impact teacher and/or student morale and other factors that affect student learning. You must constantly estimate the effects of choice on student learning.

Intended and Unintended Consequences. Alternatives are developed to solve or contribute to the solution of a problem. To properly assess their value you must identify the benefits (intended consequences) and unintended consequences. If your objective is to ensure that staff begins classes promptly and you make a choice that results in promptness (intended) and a petition to the school board (unintended), you might conclude that you achieved your objective but that you did not give proper attention to the unintended consequences. Predicting the unintended consequences is a critical component in the Best Choice equation.

Short- and Long-Term Effects. The United States has a budget deficit beyond our comprehension. For the most part, it is a result of a preoccupation with the short-term. U.S. business has suffered from the tendency to produce upward arrows on quarterly profit sheets. Similarly, the natural inclination of most principals is to place too much emphasis on short-term effects. In your world, it is today that counts. But you know the down side of that kind of thinking. Quick fixes, like aspirins, often provide short-term benefits. Unlike aspirins, they often lead to long-term illness. Long-term effects should always be considered when choosing an alternative.

Ethically Right. An ethical compass is an excellent direction finder; without it you are lost. Power, greed, and self-advancement will keep you from making the Best Choice for kids. The best way to make a good decision is to do "the right thing." The right thing is difficult to measure. There is no norm-referenced ethical standard; your standard is the only one that counts. Figure 7.1 is an ethical triangle. We have chosen fairness as a fundamental leg of the triangle. What other components would you add to the triangle to remind you that the Best Choice must be ethically right? Write down two other qualities and put up the triangle in your office.

FIGURE 7.1 ETHICAL TRIANGLE

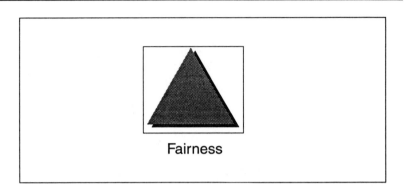

Fairness

Situation Match. The best choice fits the situation. It fits the culture, the vision, and the economic and political climate. It fits the environment and other key factors surrounding the problem. You must be very astute in determining that fit. While it may seem like you can only "feel" that fit, problem mapping, which was discussed in Chapter 5, will assist you in "feeling" your way.

CHOICE CHARTING

Ben Franklin, when making important decisions, took a piece of paper, drew a line down the middle, listed the benefits of an alternative on the left side and the unintended consequences or negative aspects on the right side. He then compared the benefits and unintended consequences and chose the alternative(s) that were most likely to achieve the goals. In this chapter, we use a modified Franklin method and walk you through Choice Charting, a two-phased process for weighting alternatives. We recommend its formal use for Elephantine problems—those high-risk big deals that you have time for and which need great attention—but we are not suggesting you use formal Choice Charting every time you solve a problem. Use the formal process when it is called for, and adopt it as a mental process to follow when making decisions.

PHASE 1 - THE PROCESS

1. Identify the problem objective.
2. Generate alternatives to meet the objective.
3. Identify benefit(s) of alternatives.
4. Identify unintended consequences of alternatives through screening.

Phase 1 begins with a clear statement of the problem; charting is impossible without it. Alternatives are then generated using the process discussed in Chapter 6. You then use five charting screens (Figure 7.2) to identify the benefits and unintended consequences in the Choice Chart (Figure 7.3).

FIGURE 7.2 CHARTING SCREENS

Sociocultural:	Demographic and cultural factors such as gender, race, ethnicity, age, beliefs, values, and norms.
Psychological:	Ways of thinking, attitudes, and emotions.
Economic:	Costs and other resources including time.
Political:	Impact or interest of influential individuals and groups.
Roles:	Impact on specific job and life roles of individuals.

Examine each alternative to determine benefits and consequences. Review the problem objective to focus on the desired outcome. As each alternative is examined, ask the " What . . . if I . . . ?" question: "What are the benefits and unintended consequences if I do . . . ?" The *sociocultural* screen will help identify culture and demographic benefits and consequences. It is im-

FIGURE 7.3 CHOICE CHART

Problem Objective(s)		
Alternatives	Benefits	Unintended Consequences
1.		
2.		
3.		
4.		
5.		
Sociocultural:	Demographic and cultural factors such as gender, race, ethnicity, age, beliefs, values, and norms.	
Psychological:	Ways of thinking, attitudes, and emotions.	
Economic:	Costs and other resources including time.	
Political:	Impact or interest of influential individuals and groups.	
Roles:	Impact on specific job and life roles of individuals.	

portant to consider the pluses and minuses that an alternative has for the affluent, the poor, minorities, young and old, etc. Screen for *psychological* consequences by thinking about how the alternative will affect peoples' attitudes and thinking. The *economic* screen requires little explanation but do not forget to identify the time costs. The longer you are in this business, the more astute you become at *political* screening; you have already learned that influentials play a significant role in determining how well or badly an alternative fares. Examine the *roles* of those involved in the problem when you consider consequences; an alternative that is beneficial for teachers can be disastrous for custodians, parents, or others. As you screen the alternatives, make notes to help you make the final judgment. When each of the objectives has been charted, move to Phase 2, Weighing Alternatives.

PHASE 2 - WEIGHING ALTERNATIVES

Determining the merits of possible solutions is tricky business. Choosing the best solution is trickier. Criteria make the decision simpler and more effective. If you are out to buy a car, you first determine the criteria. Price, gas mileage, accessories, looks, reliability, and cost typically determine your best choice. Problem solutions also have criteria. Satisfaction with outcomes, ease of implementation, and cost are typical of those examined to determine the best choice. To weigh the alternatives, choose three to five important criteria. If, for example, the problem is related to program implementation, the problem resolution criteria might be ease of implementation, cost, teacher support, and impact on instruction. If the problem is about discipline, criteria such as impact on student behavior, teacher reaction, and parent reaction are appropriate. Criteria are not typically equally weighted. When buying that car, for example, reliability may be more important to you than looks. When problem resolution criteria are unequal, simply give the total criteria 100% and weight each criterion appropriately. Ease of implementation might be assigned 40% with four other criteria 15% apiece. Figure 7.4 is a chart to enable you to weigh alternatives.

PHASE 3 - THE FINAL CHOICE

Finally, the Big Casino; making the final choice. You have sifted and sorted; now it is time to select. The Dos and Don'ts that follow guide the process. Assign them a weight, and use a holistic approach to weigh the criteria. Do not get out your calculator; weighing is different than adding. Examine the weight you have given each solution and the objective. Juggle that in your mind and then choose one alternative that best solves the problem.

FIGURE 7.4 WEIGHTING CHART

| | | RATING SCALE: 1 TO 10 | | | | |
| | | ALTERNATIVE SOLUTIONS | | | | |
CRITERIA	WEIGHT	A.	B.	C.	D.	E.
TOTAL POINTS	100%					

Do:

♦ Examine the benefits and unintended consequences.

♦ Apply each criterion to an alternative and assign it a value (for each criterion) from 1 to 10. The weight reflects your best estimate of the value of that alternative for that criterion.

♦ Holistically determine the best choice using the value of each criterion as a guide. Give credence to the most important criteria but pay attention to the others, too.

♦ If you are numbers driven, multiply the criteria weight by the value and add up the scores. This is similar to the holistic weighting, but results in a number.

♦ Choose more than one high-value alternative.

Don't:

♦ Simply add all the numbers and pick the top score. This ignores the weighting.

♦ Settle for one alternative when others have high values.

SHORTHAND VERSION

No leader in America walks around with charting guides or sits around assigning values to alternatives in solving daily problems. The process above is Elephantine, designed to solve Elephants and keep the Sharks away. Here is the D&J shorthand version for use in any problem of significance:

♦ Get your objectives clear in your head.

♦ Mentally generate as many top-quality alternatives as you can.

♦ Identify (mentally) the problem solution criteria and assign values (10-point scale) to them.

♦ Select the best choice based on value.

PRACTICE TIME

Practice makes perfect. No Such Thing as a Free Grant is a scenario that provides you the opportunity to practice charting and weighting. Alternatives have been provided. Chart them and make the best choice. We will provide feedback when you have finished.

No Such Thing as a Free Grant

For the past year, you and your staff have been working on a service learning grant. The service-learning component is for all students, but will be of special significance to students who are less academically inclined than other students. Service learning really promotes hands-on learning and is real-world. Staff is generally committed to service learning, although there are a few key teachers who oppose it. These teachers are not violently opposed to it; they seem to feel that there is too much going on and too little time. Your site council agreed that service teaming should be part of the instructional program. The PTA also supports it. Recently, several staff members, under your leadership, wrote an extensive three-year grant to generate the necessary funds to support this project. After several months of waiting, you receive a call informing you that the grant will be approved; it is big bucks. Conditions for final approval of the grant are discussed with the funding agency and seem reasonable. You announce this to the staff and PTA who appear to be very supportive and excited.

When you receive written confirmation of the grant, you learn that funding is conditional and that new compliance restrictions have been added. While you can accept first-year funding of the grant without conditions, continued funding is based on the following: (1) matching funds must be obtained from the business sector, (2) the district must provide transportation of students to community service sites, (3) a significant number of volunteer hours must be contributed by parents and community, and (4) teachers must attend summer inservice for three days with no compensation. You meet with the granting agency representatives, but they will not budge. This information is shared with the site-based council at their next meeting, when you are out of town. Using brainstorming, the council generates the alternatives below. It is a judgment call. What do you do?

Alternatives

* Decline acceptance of the grant; re-negotiate the grant
* Accept the grant for the first year only
* Seek transportation funding from business
* Select service sites students can walk to
* Seek free city transportation
* Seek volunteer hours from local service organizations
* Seek business contributions for additional funds
* Ask the district office for additional funds
* Write another grant for additional funds
* Review current site expenses to see if there are available funds
* Negotiate a lesser amount for the grant
* Seek service-learning funding from other sources
* Delay the project for an additional year, then resubmit

FEEDBACK

Begin by developing a target, the problem objective: Meet the new criteria demanded by the granting agency, move forward with the grant, and maintain support of faculty and community.

The sociocultural, economic, psychological, political, and roles screens are helpful in determining the benefits and consequences of the alternatives. The psychological benefits and unintended consequences center around impact on teacher and PTA member attitudes. A number of the alternatives have economic consequences. Securing or losing the grant obviously has economic benefits and consequences related to the granting of funds, as well as transportation and other possible costs. Because this involves the district office, the PTA, and key teachers, there are political considerations to be assessed. Finally, roles are important in this problem. Teachers, students, parents, central office, and the principal are all impacted by the choice you make.

Next, identify your problem-solving criteria:

1. Meets all grant conditions
   (a) provides transportation to students,
   (b) gets matching funds from business sector,
   (c) get volunteers,
   (d gets teacher attendance at summer institute;
2. Maintains faculty morale and support; and
3. Maintains parent support.

The best choice is to GO BACK TO THE SITE-BASED COUNCIL. This alternative is not on the list provided by the site committee. It is the best choice because none of the other choices meets all three problem-solving criteria. It appears the principal made an error in judgment by not being at that meeting. The Council's alternatives do not address the granting agency demand for three days of teacher inservice (which the teachers have not agreed to), or extended volunteer efforts from parents; there are no alternatives to produce outcomes that will meet all problem criteria. This is an all-or-nothing choice; there will be no grant unless all the problem resolutions are met. It is back to the drawing board and the site committee.

KEY BEHAVIORS

Do . . .

+ define the problem objective in specific and measurable terms.
+ identify how it will benefit students.
+ brainstorm unintended consequences.
+ decide whether it is morally or ethically right.
+ determine whether it is politically charged, economically outlandish, or has a negative cultural or psychological impact.
+ use the Choice Chart in your decision making. Add this to your planner, laptop, or think area.

DON'T . . .

- select a solution that you cannot live with.
- make a choice solely because it is safest.
- select a choice solely because it is politically correct.

FOR REFLECTION

◆ Review the big questions and determine how to call them up when needed.

◆ Ask yourself how you can use the charting screens to determine consequences.

◆ Think of effective ways to weigh choices using criteria and a holistic approach.

8

A PRACTICE CASE

Often a dash of judgment is better than a flash of genius.
—Howard W. Newton

Through seven chapters, various facets of judgment have been discussed and a number of suggestions for improving your judgment in solving school-related problems have been provided. Now is the time to apply what you learned. Spencer Elementary School is a case that is typical of problems that many principals encounter. It is an important problem and it is high stakes. Read the problem and follow the instructions provided.

Spencer Elementary School

You are the principal of Spencer Elementary School in the Spikeville School District. The district consists of ten elementary schools, two middle schools, one high school, and one 7–12 alternative school. The district is growing; its enrollment of 7,500 students has increased 30% in the past four years. The district's demographics have changed from 95% Caucasian and 5% Hispanic to 77% Caucasian, 11% Hispanic, 9% African American, 2% Asian, and 1% Native American. The percentage of students on free or reduced lunch has increased from 3% to 29%. Test scores that were once at the 88th percentile have declined and are now at the 66th percentile. Approximately 30% of the students are reading below grade level.

Student achievement has been the prime focus of Superintendent Rodney Ferguson. Dr. Ferguson, who has been
the Spikeville superintendent for the past seven years,
constantly talks about the importance of test scores and
considers them the only barometer by which to assess
the effectiveness of the educational program. Three current board members were on the board when Dr.
Ferguson was hired. They are:

> Sara Martin - 9 years on board, Board President,
>   homemaker
> Paul Davis - 8 years on board, Second Vice
>   President, physician
> Don Cantonwine - 13 years on board, farmer

The other four board members are:

> Fran Schneider - 2 years on board, banker
> Steven Ray - 5 years on board, attorney
> Martin Kowalski - 4 years on board, Vice President,
>   veterinarian
> Molly Schlephorst - 2 years on board, mail carrier

The board has shown strong support for Dr. Ferguson,
voting 7–0 on most issues. Dr. Ferguson and his wife have
a daughter who is a freshman in high school. He has
publicly stated his desire to remain in Spikeville until
his daughter's graduation. You are beginning your third
year as principal of Spencer Elementary School and have
been an employee of the district for 21 years. You taught
in Spencer for 11 years before being promoted to administration. You served as Vice Principal at Motley Middle
School and as principal at Duwell Elementary, a small
elementary school, before assuming the principalship of
Spencer Elementary.

Spencer Elementary School has 550 students, an increase
of 90 students over the past three years. It is situated on
the outskirts of town adjacent to one of Spencer's more
affluent neighborhoods. Its neighborhood is changing
quickly due to the opening of a beef packing plant not
far from the school. The school's minority population has
shown a three-year increase from 9% to 23%. Several

teaching staff have expressed concerns over the changing student body. Because the neighborhood has changed, test scores have been declining. In response to these declining test scores and because of some pressure from central office and community members, you have notified the staff that after-school tutorial sessions are to be mandatory and that they should also implement a tutorial program. After-school tutorials are within the teachers' work day, but mandating after-school instructional activities is precedent setting.

The teaching staff at Spencer has been stable. The staff has an average of 21 years' experience. The site council, which consists of four staff members, has been leading Spencer's drive toward school improvement, with the majority of staff going along with all new initiatives. Four veteran staff and the union building representative have been working against school improvement initiatives. They maintain that things had been just fine prior to your arrival. These veteran staff have been writing letters to board members about you and have sent strong letters to the site council and faculty claiming you are heavy-handed and dictatorial. You met with each of these staff members individually and discussed their concerns. These meetings were not productive; these faculty members appear convinced that you are the problem. After a recent meeting with staff in which you discussed the need for the tutorial program, you receive a call from Superintendent Ferguson.

Dr. Ferguson wants you to know that he is concerned about letters he is getting from the four faculty members. He advises you to "get them on your side." He also reaffirms his and the board's concern about declining test scores and urges you to move forward. In his words, "I and my board are solidly behind you." He does have another matter to share with you. A board member contacted him about allegations made by the district union rep. Specifically, the union rep maintained that a teacher was ready to formally charge that you were harassing her and other staff members because they would not go along with your after-school program and other "demands." The union rep reported that the teacher claims she is suffering from stress and should not be evaluated this year. She also claims your pressure tactics have made it impossible to teach effectively. The board member told the superintendent that backing off the evaluation may avoid a possible worker's compensation claim or litigation. The superintendent indicates he will leave it up to you and cautions you to be careful with all of this.

As you go through your in-basket, you encounter a memorandum from the building representative about the after-school tutorial. You pay careful attention to it because she has considerable clout with the four veteran faculty members and with other faculty members.

MEMORANDUM

DATE: September 23, 1996
TO: Terri Brown, Principal
FROM: Lynn Martin, Building Representative

This memorandum is intended to communicate the concern of this faculty with recent edicts that you have passed that infringe upon the rights of teachers and are disempowering. While I have not officially polled the staff, I have spoken to many who are very upset with the recent edict mandating after-school tutorials. They are also troubled by a leadership approach that is dictatorial and top down. Please understand that, if this recent edict is not rescinded and the style changed, we will have no choice but to formally go to the Spikeville Board of Education and the superintendent. We need to know by September 25 how you intend to proceed .

PROCESS CHECK

You sit back in your chair and think about how to respond to the memorandum and the approaches to employ in solving the problem. A five-point scale provides you an opportunity to make some judgment calls about the process to be used in solving the problem. Review the following problem-solving process and determine how important it is to use each step in solving the problem at Spencer Elementary. (Do that now. Write a number to the left of each course of action or suggestion on the list below. Finish doing that before you go to the next task).

Problem-Solving Process - Importance of Step

1 = Very important. Do it now.
2 = Somewhat important. Do it.
3 = Uncertain. Need more information.
4 = Yes and no. Depends on how you do it.
5 = No! Don't do this.

Problem-Solving Process - Practical Steps

____ Scan and reflect on the problem and determine
        its importance.
____ Focus on the problem.
____ Define the problem. Specify the problem
        objective.
____ Map the problem.
____ Generate alternatives.
____ Choose best choice(s).
____ Implement decision.

Review the steps and determine if we agree on the importance of each of the seven steps. If you score a step "1" or "2," use it in solving the problem. When you have used these steps to solve the problem, check below to compare your thinking with ours.

Scan and reflect on the problem and determine its importance: It is a big "1." You do not need radar to understand there is a problem. It involves teacher morale, the union, school improvement, and the board and superintendent. It is high stakes. You may not be sure of the number of teachers who side with the union rep and the other veteran teachers, but there is still plenty of cause for concern. The potential effects are fairly obvious. A worst case is a teacher insurrection and angry board. It is not a stretch to see something like that happen. It is an important problem.

Focus on the problem: Megadittoes; "1" again. Because it is important, it needs your full attention. Zero in on it. Clear your mind so you can think about the problem and nothing else.

Define the problem. Specify the problem objective: You should have also given this a "1." It is important to define the problem and determine what you want to achieve. We define it like this, "How do we reach agreement on the implementation of program initiatives that will raise student achievement?" We will share problem objectives later.

Map the problem: It is a "1." You cannot solve the problem without identifying the key factors. Mindmap the key factors. Changing demographics, declining test scores, the union rep, key veteran faculty members, the superintendent's perceptions and wants, the faculty, and the time urgency are important map features. Perceptions are also important. You have a sense of how the union rep and superintendent perceive matters, but you will have to consider how others see it. Obviously, there is a connection between the union rep and the four faculty members as well as between the four and the staff. There is a connection between declining test scores and the changing student population. The complainants are connected to the board. The superintendent is also connected to the board.

Generate alternatives: A "1" again! It is time to do some possibility thinking to identify the alternatives for solving your problem. We will provide alternatives later. Please add to the list as you see fit.

Best choice: This is the bottom line; "1." There is no right or easy choice. You are between the devil and the deep blue sea. Review Chapter 7, paying particular attention to the section on weighing alternatives to determine the alternative(s) that best meets the problem objective.

Implement the decision: Another "1." No judgment is final until you do something with it. The success of whatever judgment you make is contingent upon its implementation.

Practice, Practice, Practice

This is an opportunity for you to practice making judgment calls. Listed are a number of alternatives or solutions to choose from in solving the problem at Spencer Elementary. Apply the judgment criteria in determining the alternative(s) to (co)employ in solving the problem. Use the five-point scale in making a judgment call for each alternative and then make the best choice. When you finish, you will get feedback.

Problem-Solving Process - Judging Alternatives

1 = Highly effective
2 = Effective
3 = Somewhat effective
4 = Ineffective
5 = Very Ineffective

Alternatives/Solutions

____ Go see the superintendent and get his advice.
____ Meet with the building union rep.
____ Call a faculty meeting, explain the situation, and ask for their support.
____ Call a faculty meeting, explain the situation, and ask for their views.
____ Go the School Site Council and discuss the matter.
____ Ignore the memorandum.
____ Talk to key staff members to collect more information.
____ Send the faculty a memorandum explaining your rationale and approach.
____ Write a memorandum to Lynn Martin indicating your intention to proceed with the tutorial explaining why it is the best thing to do.
____ Meet with key board members.
____ Contact key parents for support.
____ Rescind the decision.
____ Back off the evaluation.

Stop! Before you can weigh the alternatives, clearly identify the problem objective(s) and the criteria for resolution. Review the case again. Write on a separate sheet of paper a statement of your objective(s) for solving this problem. Then examine your objective and see how closely it matches our problem objective.

Problem Objective: To receive sufficient support of the staff to move forward with the tutorial program and to lower resistance of key staff members to enable the program to be implemented.

The objective has two prongs. You need to move the initiative forward, but it is not enough to secure sufficient permission from the critical mass. You also have to control the negative influences of the four teachers or they will block you from getting commitment and implementing the initiative. Below are the alternatives. Weigh each of the alternatives. The criteria for resolution are listed next. You must move quickly but need more information. You cannot afford to rile up folks more, and you need more and stronger support. The problem must be contained; it could turn out to be a mess.

Problem-Solving Process - Criteria for Selecting Alternatives

- ◆ Can be done rather quickly
- ◆ Will impact student learning
- ◆ Does not inflame resistant people
- ◆ Will elicit staff support
- ◆ Will have superintendent's support
- ◆ Contains the problem

Go see the superintendent and get his advice. — No! Do not do it. You already got his advice. If you ask again you will probably be locked into whatever he "suggests." In addition, he has his own agenda and is not as close to the problem as you are. He does not know the teachers or your school as well as you. If you go to the superintendent, you also begin to establish a pattern. You identify a problem, and he solves it. He will begin to expect you to go to him. What is even worse is that you may begin to rely on someone else to solve your problems. This is your call. Make it.

Meet with the building union rep. — Do it now! Lynn Martin is a big factor. Lynn appears to be the one leading the resistance to the tutorial program. What you are doing is precedent setting, so the building rep has some leverage for blocking the approach. Lynn has clout and access to the key folks.

Call a faculty meeting, explain the situation, and ask for their support. — No! Don't do this. What would you accomplish? First, you really do not know where the faculty stands in this matter. If you conduct such a meeting you are throwing down the gauntlet and thus providing the building rep and other negative folks a chance to attack and create even more confusion or negative feeling. You are not valuing the view of the building rep. Further, you may no longer contain the problem. You do not want to do this at this point.

Call a faculty meeting, explain the situation, and ask for their views. — Yes and no. It depends on how you do it. This alternative has some merit and some shortcomings. It might work. You must set up clear ground rules; the staff must know that the purpose of the meeting is to gather information. It is probably not a good alternative. You may lose control, turning the meeting into a disaster. What will you do if it is?

Go to the School Site Council and discuss the matter. — No! Do not do it. The problem is not with the School Site Council, nor do they appear to have the ability to solve the problem. It is possible that, if things go wrong in the site council meeting, the problem will be elevated to a more serious level. You do not, in addition, have time to meet with them.

Ignore the Memorandum. — No! Do not do that. Ignoring the memorandum would be like throwing down a flaming gauntlet. Lynn's memorandum and the four resistant teachers need a response. If they do not get one, they are likely to use the lack of response to their advantage.

Talk to key staff members to collect more information. — Very effective and important. Do it now. This is a winner. You need more information. The most important thing you need to determine is the support you have within the faculty. It is the factor that drives your decision. You must identify the key faculty members to talk to and determine the level of their and others' support.

Send the faculty a memorandum explaining your rationale and approach. — *No! Do not do it.* If they have not talked to the union rep, your memo will make little sense to them. If the union rep is right, your memo will have little impact or may make things worse.

Write a memorandum to Lynn Martin indicating your intention to proceed with the tutorial explaining why it is the best thing to do. — *No! Do not do it.* Lynn has strong opinions about this and will not sit idly by while you steamroll your idea through. Chances are that it will irritate Lynn and make things worse.

Meet with key board members. — *No! Do not do it.* This is not a board problem. Yet, it might be if you get them involved. The more you have board members involved in a matter of this kind, the worse it gets. We put their names in the scenario to distract you. Do not get caught up in trying to "be political" unless you have to.

Contact key parents for support. — *No! Do not do it.* This is not a parent problem, nor is their support of any value at this point. You may not need their support if you handle this problem well. Suppose you do get the support and the teachers are threatened by it? You need teacher support first.

Rescind the tutorial choice. — *No! Do not do it.* We sure hope you did not identify rescinding the tutorial as a good choice. First, if the tutorial is worth doing, you'd better figure out how to make it work. Next, it does not seem necessary to abort this mission. What will the teachers who support the initiative think if you back off an important approach for improving student achievement?

Back off the evaluation. — No! Do not do it. The information you have provides nothing to indicate that the evaluation has anything to do with the memorandum. We put this in the case as a distraction.

BEST CHOICE

This is a relatively simple judgment call. There are only three alternatives that have merit.

1. Talk to key staff members to collect more information.
2. Meet with building union rep.
3. Call a faculty meeting, explain the situation, and ask for their views.

Talking to key staff members is the best alternative; more information as to how staff perceives this problem is needed. If you can schedule it quickly, we would suggest you do that first. You have a day or two to talk to key staff members and determine where you stand. You need to collect more information to determine your next step. When you have determined key folks to provide insight into how the faculty views this problem and have also determined what questions you will ask to get the information you need, you then examine the other alternatives before making your next judgment call. This is quite common. Also attempt to identify more alternatives through your discussions with key faculty members.

Meeting with Lynn, the building rep, provides an opportunity to change the timetable and better understand Lynn's position. A lack of time to solve the problem before it escalates is a concern. Persuade Lynn to back off the time frame so you will have some room to operate. In addition, learning more about what is bothering Lynn may enable you to do or say something that allows you to move forward. There are a number of ways to do this should you choose to. You might send a memorandum explaining that you need more time or go and talk to Lynn and explain the need for more time. This meeting could also exacerbate the problem if not handled well or if the rep is not open to discussion. You will have to handle this well.

The meeting with the faculty to gather more information may follow the first two alternatives. Or it may not. After meeting with key staff members and Lynn, you ought to know if meeting with staff to get more information is a good idea. In most cases, it would seem advisable. It is usually a matter of timing and the quality of their relationship with you.

Let us review. To make a good judgment call in solving this problem, we considered the sequence and timing of events and cause-effect relationships. Weigh each alternative in light of its probable consequences. Knowing when and how to implement the chosen alternative holds the key to their success. There are shades of gray in most alternatives. That is another reason why judgment calls are challenging.

KEY BEHAVIORS

Do . . .

+ make a commitment to improving your judgment.
+ write it down.
+ review it during your think time.
+ take time to reflect on your progress and assess your new skills.
+ revise your plan.
+ repeat the above.

DON'T . . .

- abandon the process.

FOR REFLECTION

How will you practice improving your judgment? Identify at least one person who can give you feedback on your thinking and judgment; ask this person to be a critical friend.

9

FINAL THOUGHTS

Expect the best.

The opportunity to make a judgment call that enriches the life of a young person is a very special privilege. Most educators derive great satisfaction from their work because they enjoy the ripple effect that comes with making a difference. This last chapter helps to pull things together so that you can make even more waves. We summarize the important models and distill previously provided information for ready reference. Some key behaviors and how to's are also detailed. We then hit you with Action TNT, suggestions for doing it Today, Not Tomorrow.

READY REFERENCE

MODELS/APPROACHES

Models and schemes provide conceptual frameworks and guide thinking. They should be part of your thinking and the way you make judgments. Let us review the models and approaches presented in this book and consider how they help you make waves. The *Seven-Step Problem-Solving Framework* is a sensible approach to problem solving that will increase your effectiveness. Make two copies of the model (Appendix A, or Figure 2.1); put one in your planner and the other where you can see it daily.

The *SSFM Model* (Appendix B, or Figure 5.1) is an effective approach for using the problem-solving framework. *Scan* the environment, and find problems before they find you. Then *Screen* the problem using jurisdiction, adequacy of information, urgency, importance, timing, and readiness to determine whether to discard, defer, decide, or diagnose and decide (*4D Problem Screening Guide*, Appendix C, or Figure 5.3). *Focus* enables the problem solver to hone in with intensity. Finally, *Mapping* provides the vehicle for identifying people, action/events, sequence, timing, perceptions, assumptions, beliefs, values, cause and effect, key factors, and relationships within the problem with sufficient specificity to effectively analyze the problem (*Problem Mapping Guide*, Appendix D, or Figure 5.4).

Choice Charting is a systematic way to make tough decisions (Appendix E, or Figure 7.3). Five screens (sociocultural, psychological, economic, political, and roles) provide a logical way to weigh the benefits of alternatives against unintended consequences to make the best choice. The chart for weighing alternatives is Appendix F (Figure 7.4). The *Mental Process in Judgment* (Appendix G, or Figure 2.3) is the right way to think through a problem. Mentally search your memory bank for facts and ideas, and conduct an environmental scan to add to that information. Juggle those facts and ideas, seeking to understand the problem. Ask "What if" questions, and conduct thought experiments. Then use reasoning to reach conclusions as to what will work best. Do it, evaluate the outcome, and deposit what you learned from the experience in your memory bank for future reference.

CREATIVITY

The best judgments come from the best alternatives. To generate the best alternatives, crank up your creativity. The most effective ways to crank up your creativity is to control your self-talk and make that inner voice work *for* you. Remind yourself frequently that creativity is mind over matter. Tell your inner voice to let you into the right side of your brain. Ask "What if?" frequently and let your mind wander or run amok. Play word games with yourself. Identify a problem, and then write down the first ten ideas that come to mind. Relax a moment; write down ten more. See how many of those words can be paired to create something else. Then see if any of these ideas can be used to solve the problem. Sounds crazy, does it not? Wonder why it works? Cranking up your creativity works. Expand your horizons, and become a voracious learner. Schedule think time. Schedule time for idea creation. Make time for sitting or lying down and hatching new ideas. Then think about the ideas and how exciting they are. Play more. Laugh more. Dream more. Worry less.

REMEMBERING

Memory plays a significant role in judgment because it provides facts and ideas the brain uses to make judgment calls. While some people appear to have an innate ability to store and retain information, you are likely to enhance your memory by adopting specific strategies hooked to two basic principles: (1) information can be encoded in ways that increase memory capacity, and (2) the way things are remembered is a function of the meaning given to them. There are three ways to ensure that deposits in the memory bank are stored so they can be recalled.

Mnemonics, repetition, and use. If there is specific information that you want to remember, encode it in a way that enables you to remember it. Arrange key words in such a way that their first letters represent the words or concepts you want to remember. We want you to remember Scanning, Screening, Focusing, and Mapping in the order they should be utilized so we labeled the approach the SSFM Model. Now we will use another strategy, repetition. SSFM: Scanning, Screening, Focusing and Mapping. Your brain, unlike a copy machine, makes imprints more deeply each time it records them. The more frequently the brain deals with a fact or idea, the more likely it is to recall it. You are more likely to remember these four because we repeated them. If you want to remember names, events, or concepts, repeat or replay them in your mind. Finally, there is an element of truth to the old saying, "use it or lose it." The use of a fact or idea facilitates memory. You are more likely to remember a number if you dial it than if you only think about it or say it aloud. Mnemonics, repetition, and use each aid memory. In combination, they are powerful ways to make deposits in your memory bank that can be withdrawn to make high-stakes calls.

Meaning. Remembering is an associative activity. Answer these two questions: Where were you and what were you doing on November 22, 1963? What were you doing last Friday? Most people remember what they were doing on that date in 1963, but cannot tell you what they were doing last Friday. That is because President John F. Kennedy was *not* assassinated last Friday. When facts or ideas are associated with things that have meaning, we are more likely to remember them. When you want to remember something, link it to things that have meaning to you. Associating Sharks with urgent and important problems and labeling the other types accordingly helps you remember the type of problem and how to classify it.

Rehearsal Thinking. Rehearsal thinking is a form of internal scanning. Imagine that you have many bins stuffed with facts and ideas, but you do not know what is in those bins. Rehearsing what you are going to do or say directs a search to bins where ideas associated with that event are stored. It is a form of data snooping. Rehearsing strategy by thinking through it unconsciously promotes snooping into bins related to the problem and uncovers pieces of memory that are needed to reason.

MINDMAPPING

Mindmapping is a great strategy for problem mapping. A Mindmap is an idea map; it represents relationships between ideas using symbols or words. A Mindmap allows you to think about a subject from many angles and reinforces the visual learner. More importantly, it allows your brain to do what it does best: make meaning out of fragmented pieces. Your brain is much more comfortable discovering patterns than linear relationships. You can use the Post-it, that wonderful invention of 3M, to represent connections and relationships graphically. Main ideas are centrally located, with other relationships and interrelationships depicted. Write down your ideas on Post-its and then put them up where your brain can scan them. That big picture view will stimulate Level 2 thinking. When you coordinate the big picture with its details, your right and left brain work as partners in whole brain processing. The big picture with details enables your brain to process, store, and recall information more efficiently. There are four Mindmapping steps:

1. On a Post-it, specify your problem in the form of a question: How do I work with Bill more effectively? Put the Post-it on a board or space where you can place other Post-its.

2. Examine the problem question, and generate ideas to solve the problem. Put an idea on a Post-it and place it on the board. Continue placing ideas on the board until you are out of ideas. It helps to continue to examine your ideas as you are generating new ones.

3. Examine your ideas. Put together similar ideas by moving the Post-its around. Determine how you can synthesize like ideas into big ideas and how to put big ideas together. Hang onto the little ideas you like.

4. Put together a plan with the big and little ideas.

MESS MAPPING

Mess mapping is an approach that can be used when you have a problem that is convoluted or so messy you do not know where to begin. Some problems resemble the proverbial rat's nest; they are so snarled it is difficult to know where to start to unravel them. When those problems appear, we need a way to step back and see some of the loose ends. We also need a good way to pull these loose ends apart. Mess mapping, an approach similar to mindmapping, is specifically designed to aid understanding of complex problems. Review the process:

1. *Identify the mess generally* — Write down a label for the mess using three words or less: Students Protesting.

2. *Perfect world* — Identify the perfect world without the mess. Draw a circle around the mess and enter the attributes of the perfect world using Post-its: satisfied students, happy parents, better teacher morale, positive public relations, happy superintendent, etc.

3. *Identify major mess components* — Draw an outlying circle and write each major component of the mess (e.g., cafeteria, rules, communication) on its own Post-it.

4. *Identify influencers of each component* — On separate Post-its list the cause and effect of each mess component. Array them around the relevant component.

5. *Identify factors or recent changes for influencers* — List changes that have created these influencers.

6. *Prioritize influencers and changers* — Color code them so that the most important stand out.

7. *Analyze major impact items* — Determine what is happening and why.

8. *Brainstorm solutions* — You can now identify solutions hooked to components and influencers.

AN OPEN MIND

A closed mind is the most common cause of poor judgment. Mindsets, bias, and other similar thinking afflictions close us off from collecting and analyzing data and ideas. They create reasoning roadblocks. Some equate an open mind with being wishy-washy. There is no virtue in ignoring facts and ideas. How can you double check your facts or logic if your closed mind will not let you? There are some basic principles that will help you keep your mind open:

♦ STOP, LOOK, and LISTEN whenever you encounter contradictions; they may indicate false facts or flawed thinking.

♦ Check and verify facts.

♦ Ask yourself and others for contrary facts, viewpoints, or opinions; listen for feedback and for more information.

LEVEL 2 THINKING

Level 2 thinking is at that problem-solving zone where you are focused on achievement and constantly scanning, screening, processing, and analyzing information to solve routine and high-stakes problems. The most effective leaders think at Level 2 most of the time; they know it is the Zone of Effectiveness. Most tell us that they take pride in having developed the ability to operate at Level 2. They are proud of their ability to focus and think well. Here are some suggestions for operating at Level 2 on a daily basis.

♦ *Attack.* Attack problems. Go get them before they get you. View them as a chance to make even more of a difference and as an opportunity to demonstrate, practice, and hone your skill. Think of problem solving as an opportunity to do something at which you are really good. Here are two dynamite questions to frame the attack.

What is great about this problem?

What is exciting about this problem?

♦ *30-Second Drill.* Treat every problem as a potential gold mine or disaster for at least 30 seconds. Focus on it with intensity. Screen it to determine if it is a Shark or an Elephant. Tune in the Sharks and Elephants; tune out the Mice. Try to delegate the Coyotes.

♦ *Ask Yourself Questions.* Thinking is the process of asking yourself questions and answering them. When you ask a question, you are moving toward the second level. Thinking causes you to evaluate and create— the two most important Level 2 activities. Be sure to ask yourself how you are thinking when solving a problem.

♦ *Cogitate, Incubate, Iterate.* Ideas and solutions are like your body; they require attention. Some problems require a deep massage. More correctly, they require thinking, incubating, and rethinking. If you stay with an important problem and continue running through the factors, connections, causes, effects, and possibilities, it is not uncommon to have an AHA! This is particularly true of political problems marked by webs of intriguing relationships and motivations. It is surprising and sometimes embarrassing to suddenly have it dawn on you that the reason Mr. Smith suggested something is because it will benefit Mr. X. That best choice for tough problems often comes after several iterations of thinking. The art of beating something to death rests on your ability to limit this type of thinking to a small number of high-stakes problems.

♦ *Intuit.* How do you put this all together so that it becomes a natural, free-flowing, skillful act? Intuition plays a significant role in judgment. Tacit knowledge and commitment interact to produce an automatic response reflecting your knowledge and feelings. Keep learning and practicing.

CONTROL

You must control yourself and the problem-solving process, but far too frequently your day goes something like this — shut off the alarm, grab a quick breakfast, give and receive a peck on the cheek, buzz to the office, and shake hands with your persistent friends known as problems, crises, conflicts, and calendar changes. It is little wonder that more than half of today's principals report feeling harried or overwhelmed. Educational journals dedicate entire issues to stress, time management, health maintenance, and psychology. This makes some sense; each is related to mental health and attitudes. But problems play a more potent role in determining your mental health and stress level. They promote a sense of powerlessness and helplessness.

Control and efficacy are the antidotes to helplessness. Accept that solving problems is what you do, so take control of all aspects of the problem. When you feel powerless, stress level rises and effectiveness suffers. It is as if you have fallen into quicksand and cannot get out. Waiting for the rescue is not fun. Most of us are inclined to paddle like heck, get in deeper, and begin to believe that the problem is permanent (not temporary), pervasive (everything is wrong), and personal (it's ME). We become helpless.

You cannot control the number of problems that come your way (although you can prevent a number of them), but you can control how you think and how you attack problems. Control the priority you give each problem, the time you spend on specific problems, and the manner in which you handle problems. Attacking problems systematically and tactically leads to success and to self-efficacy. Self-efficacy is a set of beliefs about one's own ability to organize and execute courses of action required to maintain designated types of performances. Research by Bandura over more than two decades has proven that the greater a person's task ability, the greater that person's self-efficacy and the more likely that person is to experience further increases in ability. The bottom line: the better you become at problem solving, the better you feel about yourself, which leads to increased skill and more efficacy — a virtuous cycle. Get caught in this virtuous cycle.

REASONING ROADBLOCKS

The eight reasoning roadblocks are worth remembering. Failure to negotiate them results in faulty reasoning. Store them in your memory banks for instant use. Think JIF CHILI and the three information I's. When we omit information, block it out, or drift because of it, reasoning suffers. That leaves JF and CHL. Jumping to conclusions blocks and omits information, and False Facts mess up your reasoning because the information is not accurate. Now CHL. Reasoning demands that you make the proper Connections and that you keep your Hot Buttons under control. Finally, if your Logic is Loose your reasoning will be Lousy. Note the eight roadblocks and some ways to control for them. See Figure 9.1

FIGURE 9.1 REASONING ROADBLOCKS

Roadblock	Reminder
J umping to conclusions	Count to 10
I nformation Block	Open your mind
F alse Facts	Verify, verify
C onnection Failure	Map
H ot Buttons	Stay Cool
I nformation Drift	Make up mind
L oose logic	Tighten thinking
I nformation Omission	Scan, scan

STYLE

There are two worlds. One has facts, numbers, details, and rules. The other we feel with our heart and emotions. Do you process information with your head or your heart? We have argued in this book that the most effective approach to problem solving employs processing in a systematic way. You sift and sort in a systematic way. We have also argued that the more expertise one has, the more one is intuitive. But the person making the judgment call has to choose a style and use it consistently. Here are three suggestions to guide you.

1. Do not confuse emotion and intuition. If a judgment call feels wrong because you are scared or mad, that is not intuition, it is emotion. When that sixth sense called intuition checks in, trace it backward to determine the source of the feeling. If that feeling emanates from an emotion that is interfering with reasoning, do your best to discount it.

2. Use intuition and reasoning by "thinking backward" and "thinking forward." Think backward by looking for patterns and making links as well as trying to see the big picture and how things in that picture are connected. Think forward by determining cause and effect, identifying problem solution criteria, and weighing the alternatives.

3. Accept that judgment calls can be made systematically *and* rapidly. It is simply a matter of expertise and practice. Slow does not mean systematic. Some people take a long time wandering around a problem. Fast does not mean intuitive. The very best decision makers are systematic in their approach to high stakes problems.

ACTION TNT

In *Empires of the Mind,* Denis Waitley (1995) used Action TNT in the context of time management. It has a broader use, life management. Consider these suggestions for moving you from thinking about it to just doing it.

HABITS OF MIND

Your belief system provides the foundation for growth and development. Improving your judgment requires powerful habits of mind. Several habits of mind are essential for excellence in exercising judgment. Make them your habits of mind:

♦ A belief that judgment is an essential skill that can be improved upon

♦ A belief in the problem-solving model and judgment strategies and their use

♦ An understanding of how you create ideas and a belief in their importance

♦ A dislike of arrogance in your thinking and an affinity for that balance between confident thinking and humility

♦ A commitment to Level 2 thinking and to what it will take to achieve and maintain that level

♦ A belief in being flexible in your thinking and a commitment to utilizing the principles of the Six Hats approach

♦ An understanding of the power of reasoning and a commitment to reason well

♦ A commitment to continuous improvement of the skills and attributes that contribute to judgment

COMMIT TO ACHIEVEMENT

When picking a team, always look for those who love to win and hate to lose. Achievement-oriented leaders make good judgment calls because they love success and cannot stand failure. Activity-oriented leaders (an oxymoron) do not worry much about judgment calls; just moving around the swamp satisfies their need. Politically oriented leaders (a worse oxymoron) make judgment calls that are good for them but not necessarily good for kids. You cannot make a good judgment call unless you know what you want to achieve and are committed to results. Where you want to go drives or pervades every judgment call. Put your mission statement and goals where they are accessible. Examine them from time to time, especially when you face high stakes decisions.

COMMIT TO PROCESS

Processes are a series of actions or operations that lead toward a particular result. Processes are easier to discern when they deal with production of widgets than they are when they deal with ideas or human behavior. Leadership revolves around your ability to skillfully employ a number of important technical and people processes. Making judgment calls is a process, not a series of unrelated activities. In this book, we have provided approaches that enable you to use specific strategies in a systematic way. The more you understand, refine, and practice the use of the processes, the more skillful you will become. You will not only be able to utilize the processes more skillfully in routine problem solving, you will be able to adapt them to handle unique problems. The approaches we have provided are described earlier in this chapter and are in the appendices. Revisit them, streamline them if it helps, and find a way to use them routinely. You may want to use 3X5 cards or put something in your planner until it becomes part of your thinking and routine. Commit to it. Stick with it. Think more about it, use it, think some more, refine it so it works for you.

REFLECT, REFLECT, REFLECT

The peerless judge reflects or thinks deeply before, during, and after practice. *Reflection before practice* provides an opportunity to think about the process and tactics that will be used as well as how you are thinking about the problem and other things that will affect your judgment. Olympic athletes, surgeons, and other professionals prepare for important events by sealing themselves off and getting into the proper mental state. When it is high stakes time for you, find a few minutes to reflect on your thinking and the processes you will use to solve the problem.

Reflection during practice, sometimes known as reflection in action or "thinking on your feet," means that you think about how you are solving the problem while doing it. As you sit there with the parent who is still dissatisfied, review the problem-solving model and tactical approaches and examine your thinking to determine what to do to solve the problem. It may force you to reexamine your objectives and thinking and to develop a new approach. Reflection during practice often results in two very important outcomes: (1) you learn about practice and your performance because you are studying it while doing it, and (2) you perform better because you are analyzing aspects of the process as well as making judgments and taking action on both the judgment process and the problem.

Reflection after practice provides the optimum time to critique and improve the process and further develop your skills. When you reflect after making a tough judgment call, ask yourself four questions: (1) How effectively did I utilize the various aspects of the problem-solving model? (2) What aspect of the problem-solving process do I need to improve? (3) How was I thinking and what aspect of my thinking do I need to improve upon or change? (4) What did I do well that I need to feel good about and continue to do?

PRACTICE THE ETHICS OF EXCELLENCE

Excellence is a process and a state of mind. You cannot be the best without demonstrating fairness, integrity, principles, and high standards. You have to go beyond the letter of the law reflected in state statute or education code. You have to sweat the small stuff because integrity is about little things as well as big ones. High-stakes decisions are all too frequently complicated by ethical dilemmas: What if the student is right but the teacher will cause problems for you if not supported? What if teacher candidate X is minimally qualified while Y is excellent, but a board member would appreciate it if X got the job? The answer to the first question is a tradeoff or compromise; the second has no wiggle room. Remind yourself of the ethics of excellence; hold yourself accountable for doing what is right, not what merely makes people happy. Put your judgment calls to the "60 Minute Test"; when you make a decision, be willing to defend it on *60 Minutes* with Mike Wallace in your face.

COMMIT TO GROWTH

The demand for adaptability in educational leadership has reached an astoundingly high level. We are experiencing an unprecedented explosion of knowledge. Instability, uncertainty, complexity, increased diversity, technology, a global environment, and heightening value conflicts pose persistent and unique problems demanding multiple solutions. Judgment is the currency of the realm in uncertain times when the stakes are high. Here is a two-part growth plan to meet that challenge:

1. *Widen your knowledge level through reading.* Reading is still the most efficient method for acquiring knowledge. The stress of daily business and long hours places tremendous demands on you. Yet your effectiveness in analyzing a problem and in finding solutions is significantly affected by your knowledge level. The more you know about the problem content, the better you are at identifying and understanding the important factors and the more effective you are at generating alternative solutions. Can you read something that will contribute to your growth for one hour every other day plus a couple of hours extra on the weekend? If you are like most people, you are awake approximately 110 hours during a week. If you commit to reading four hours a week, you will read for more than 200 hours per year, the equal of 25 days. It will make a difference.

2. *Set a growth goal related to judgment.* Throughout this book we have encouraged you to participate in various growth activities. This one is really simple. Iden-

tify the single most important thing you could work on in the next 12 months that would improve your judgment. Think of the concepts and ideas related to problem solving and judgment, do a needs assessment to identify what would be most important for you to work on, then develop a plan. Develop a specific objective, strategies to achieve the objective, and ways to monitor progress and results. Then specify the timelines. The final step is to find a way or a person to help you carry out your plan.

You Can Do It

How do you get to Carnegie Hall from here? Rehearse! Rehearse! Rehearse! In today's world, tears may get you sympathy, but only sweat will get you change. Perseverance is more powerful than talent. Commit to these three very powerful words — **EXPECT THE BEST.** If you are anticipating the worst while hoping for the best, you will usually get the worst. Expect the best and you will get the best. Save the highest expectations for yourself. When you get up each morning expecting the very best of yourself, you will be hard to stop. The greatest challenge that human beings face is to give up what they are to become all that they are capable of becoming. Excellence is not something you find, it is something you create.

Key Behavior

JUST DO IT!

APPENDIX A

The Seven-Step Problem-Solving Framework

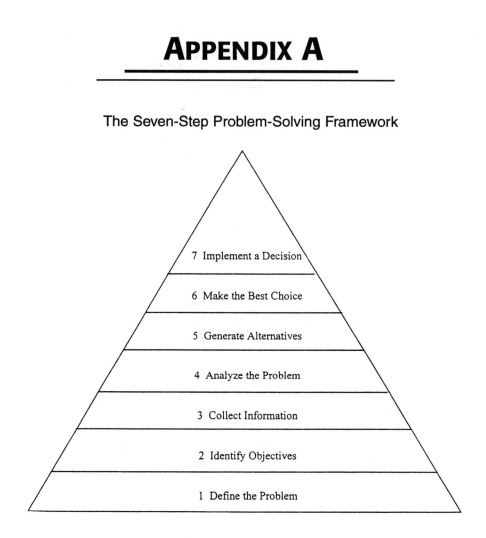

7 Implement a Decision

6 Make the Best Choice

5 Generate Alternatives

4 Analyze the Problem

3 Collect Information

2 Identify Objectives

1 Define the Problem

APPENDIX B

SSFM Model

Scanning   Monitor environment to recognize problems

Screening   Filter problem to determine problem priority

Focusing   Hone in on problem with intensity

Mapping   Break problem down to determine connection
between problem elements

APPENDIX C

4D Problem Screening Guide

Screen	**Key Question**
Jurisdiction	Is it my problem?
Adequacy of Information	Do I have sufficient information?
Urgency	How urgent is it?
Importance	How important is it?
Timing	Is now the time?
Readiness	Am I emotionally ready?

Problem Choices	
Discard	Do not deal with problem.
Defer	Address problem at a later time.
Decide	Make judgment call.
Diagnose/Decide	Collect and analyze information, then decide.

APPENDIX D

Problem Mapping Guide

Problem Elements	Big Questions
People	Who is involved and in what way?
Actions/Events	What actions and/or events occurred?
Sequence	What was the order or sequence of actions and events?
Timing	When did actions/events occur, and when did people do whatever they did?
Perceptions	How do individuals and groups view the matter?
Assumptions, Beliefs	What assumptions, beliefs, values, and attitudes have impact?
Cause/Effect	What are the causes-effect relationships, and why did certain events and actions cause problems?
Key Factors	What are the key factors to be considered in better understanding the problem?
Relationships	What are the relationships among key factors, people, perceptions, actions, events, time, sequence, and cause and effect?

APPENDIX E

Choice Chart

Problem Objective(s): _____

Alternatives	Benefits	Unintended Consequences
1.		
2.		
3.		
4.		
5.		
6.		
7.		
8.		
9.		
10.		

Sociocultural:	Demographic and cultural factors such as gender, race, ethnicity, age, beliefs, values, and norms.
Psychological:	Ways of thinking, attitudes, and emotions.
Economic:	Costs and other resources including time.
Political:	Impact or interest of influential individuals and groups.
Roles:	Impact on specific job and life roles of individuals.

APPENDIX F

Weighting Chart

		RATING SCALE: 1 TO 10				
		ALTERNATIVE SOLUTIONS				
		A.	B.	C.	D.	E.
CRITERIA	WEIGHT					
TOTAL POINTS	100%					

APPENDIX G

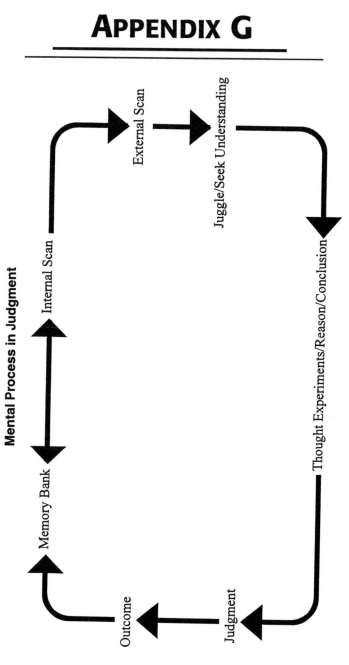

Mental Process in Judgment

Internal Scan

External Scan

Juggle/Seek Understanding

Thought Experiments/Reason/Conclusion

Memory Bank

Outcome

Judgment

REFERENCES

Bacharach, S. B. (1990). *Education reform: Making sense of it all.* Needham Heights, MA: Allyn & Bacon.

Brookfield, S. D. (1989). *Developing critical thinkers.* San Francisco, CA: Jossey-Bass.

Caplow, T. (1983). *Managing an organization.* New York: CBS College.

Carr, C., & Fletcher, M. (1990). *The manager's troubleshooter.* Englewood Cliffs, NJ: Prentice-Hall.

Chang, R., & Kelly, K.(1995). *Step-by-step problem solving.* Irvine, CA: Richard Chang Associates.

Costa, A. L. (1985). *Developing minds.* Alexandria, VA: Association for Supervision and Curriculum Development.

Covey, S. R. (1989). *The 7 habits of highly effective people.* New York: Simon & Schuster.

Dawson, R. (1993). *The confident decision maker.* New York: William Morrow.

de Bono, E. (1970). *Lateral thinking.* New York: Harper & Row.

de Bono, E. (1982). *de Bono's thinking course.* UK: Facts on File.

de Bono, E. (1990). *The mechanism of mind.* New York: Penguin.

de Bono, E. (1992A). *Serious creativity.* New York: Harper Business.

de Bono, E. (1992B). *Sur/Petition (going beyond competition).* New York: Harper Business.

Drucker, P. F. (1993). *Management: Tasks, responsibilities, practices.* New York: Harper & Row.

Ehringer, A. G. (1995). *Make up your mind.* Santa Monica, CA: Merritt.

Goleman, D. (1995). *Emotional intelligence.* New York: Bantam Books.

Hanks, K., & Parry, J. (1991). *Wake up your creative genius.* Menlo Park, CA: Crisp.

Hogarth, R. A. (1980). *Judgment and choice: The psychology of decision.* Chichester, NY: John Wiley & Sons.

Jenkins, D., & Stout, G. (1995). *The best American sports writing 1995*. New York: Houghton Mifflin.

Kepner, C., & Tregoe, B. (1965). *The rational manager*. New York: McGraw-Hill.

Kline, P., & Saunders, B. (1993). *Ten steps to a learning organization*. Arlington, VA: Great Ocean.

Lindblom, C. E. (1959). The science of muddling through. *Public Administrative Review, 19,* 79-99.

Mowen, J. C. (1993). *Judgment calls*. New York: Simon & Schuster.

Newman, J. (1992). *How to stay cool, calm & collected when the pressure's on*. New York: AMACOM.

Noone, D. J. (1993). *Creative problem solving*. New York: Barron's Educational Series.

Pound, R., & Pritchett, P. (1995). *The stress of organizational change*. Dallas, TX: Pritchett & Associates.

Pritchett, P. (1993). *Culture shift*. Dallas, TX: Pritchett & Associates.

Quinlivan-Hall, D., & Renner, P. (1994). *In search of solutions*. San Diego, CA: Pfeiffer.

Rogers, H. C. (1984). *Rogers' rules for success*. New York: St. Martin's/Marek.

Ruchlis, H. (1990). *Clear thinking*. Buffalo, NY: Prometheus Books.

Schën, D. A. (1983). *The reflective practitioner*. New York: Basic Books.

Senge, P. (1990). *The fifth discipline: The art & practice of the learning organization*. New York: Doubleday.

Senge, P., Roberts, C., Ross, R. B., Smith, B. J., & Kleiner, A. (1994). *The fifth discipline fieldbook*. New York: Doubleday.

Simon, H. A. (1976). *Administrative behavior*. New York: The Free Press.

Thomson, S. (1993). *Principles for our changing schools: Knowledge and skillbase*. Fairfax, VA: National Policy Board for Educational Administration.

Tobin, D. R. (1996). *Transformational learning*. New York: John Wiley & Sons.

Waitley, D. (1995). *Empires of the mind*. New York: William Morrow.

Wells, T. (1980). *Keeping your cool under fire*. New York: McGraw-Hill.

Wonder, J., & Donovan, P. (1984). *Whole brain thinking*. New York: William Morrow.

Wycoff, J. (1991). *Mindmapping*. New York: Berkley.

Wycoff, Joyce (1995). *Transformation thinking*. New York: Berkley.